WHEN ARE YOU COMING HOME?

WHEN ARE YOU COMING HOME?

A Personal Guide to Soul Transcendence

JOHN-ROGER, DSS
with PAULI SANDERSON, DSS

MANDEVILLE PRESS
Los Angeles, California

M

MANDEVILLE PRESS
P.O. Box 513935
Los Angeles, CA 90051-1935
jrbooks@mandevillepress.org
www.mandevillepress.org

Printed in the United States of America
ISBN 1-893020-23-1

CONTENTS

ACKNOWLEDGMENTS

Our heartfelt thanks go to the following people for helping to make this book happen:

John Morton for his encouragement on day one of this project to write "a book about soul." Lisa Loewner and Scott Robinson for providing "outside eyes" and their thoughtful and intelligent perspectives. John Cawley, Stephen Keel, Nancy O'Leary, Carrie Hopkins, Marie Leighton, and Betsy Alexander for taking the book to its final steps. Vincent Dupont for his guidance through all the many stages of production. Shelley Noble and David Sand for their designing talents. Peter Sanderson for his unflagging support and love.

WHEN ARE YOU COMING HOME?

And God spoke to the soul of His beloved child words of His longing and His love, of His desire to put aside separation and to welcome His child home to the magnificence of spirit realms. "When are you coming home?" God whispered, "When are you coming home?"

And in the world called Earth, the child heard that whisper in a place so deep within himself, he hadn't even known of its existence. The child's soul stirred and began to come awake. It reached out for God's words and for the radiance of Light that shone through the words and for the home it had left so long ago. This soul yearned to know its true nature and to claim its heritage. It embraced loving and learned that its sustenance was love, peace, and joy. The soul's journey was not a quick one, but the homecoming was magnificent.

A GUIDE FOR SOUL TRANSCENDENCE

John-Roger's story—the subject of this book—is the story of one man's spiritual journey. He tells us of his journey, not only through this life but through other lives, part of what he calls his "far memory." But the greater story may be that from his personal journey was born a philosophy of Soul Transcendence—or, if you will, a science of Soul Transcendence that he has been teaching for nearly forty years to students all over the world.

Through his story, like an explorer, he shares his observations and maps some of the territory for us. He points out some key signposts for us to look for in our own journey, giving us lots of tips for our travels. In his story we can find principles for creating our own successful adventures. What began as his personal quest to find his way home to God and the Spirit within himself expanded into a guide for others who also want to find their way home. That's what this book is about. Of course, you may simply decide to "come along for the ride" and enjoy the stories of John-Roger's spiritual journey. In either case, let your experience be your guide—for, ultimately, the answers are within you.

The hallmark of Soul Transcendence is its simplicity. Soul Transcendence, as John-Roger presents it, is becoming aware of yourself as a soul and as one with God, not as a theory but as a living reality. John-Roger relates to the soul as who you truly are; it is more than your body, your thoughts, or your feelings. It is the highest aspect of yourself, where you and God are one.

Soul Transcendence requires only a willingness to commit to loving, to trust, and to expansion—and to live life consciously and with awareness. There are no gimmicks. Soul Transcendence can be practiced by anyone. It isn't a religion. It's a way of relating to yourself. It's a recognition that you are a child of God and divine in your very nature. It is a way of seeing life from the perspective of your soul. And from that perspective, life becomes a never-ending adventure. Everything is apt to take on new meaning. The ordinary remains ordinary, yet it takes on a new quality of discovery. Routine activities become the backdrop for expressions of the soul. Life's smallest challenges (or largest) can transform themselves from problems that drag you down into opportunities to practice loving, peace, or kindness—qualities of the soul you'll hear more about in John-Roger's story. Ultimately, Soul Transcendence is a journey unfolding in ways that may seem unfamiliar at first but that gradually grow and blossom in a manner that is both uniquely personal and on purpose for you.

In his story, you'll hear about several different teachers John-Roger studied with in this life. He also shares about guides who appeared to him in his inner experiences. And beyond the obvious beings who stood in as teachers, John-Roger demonstrates an attitude of openness—and even adventure—to discovering "teachers" in the lessons of life everywhere. The chapters of his story are not sequenced in exact chronological order. Rather, they follow themes of spiritual unfoldment. As John-Roger himself points out, these stories are a distillation of a long and gradual personal progression. Readers sometimes view spiritual advancement as a dramatic event that an exalted being attains. Actually, the awakening is usually more gradual. It is more the result of consistent application of awareness and attention, of a continuing series of choices often encountered in the setting of ordinary living.

Soul Transcendence, then, is about choosing. Choosing love over hate. Choosing peace over againstness. Choosing kindness over harshness. Choosing hope over despair. Life presents many "games" of struggling and stress. Within us is the soul, holding the keys to our fulfillment. Using these keys, we can play a new game by bringing love into all expressions of life. That's the game of love. When you're in the game of life, but consciously choose to play the game of love, you are practicing Soul Transcendence.

Let's hear John-Roger's story.

CHAPTER ONE

HEARING THE FATHER'S CALL
TO COME HOME TO GOD

ONE

I'm going to tell you a story. It includes bits and pieces of my journeys, my spiritual travels in this and other worlds, in this and other times. It is a story of separation physically, emotionally, spiritually, and it is a story of returning to myself and to my God.

In this story, I am myself, and in some ways, I am also everyman. I might be of any race or creed, of any color or condition. I might be male or female. I am simply human and, thus, a child of God.

Through my journeys, I have discovered that our souls are sparks of the divine—God individualized. Our souls are our connection to God and to Spirit. When we rise high enough, all our souls are of the same essence, and so we are all connected. We are all one. We are all of divine Spirit.

In the journeys of my lives, I have come to believe that the suffering of humankind lies in its perceived separation from God, which is the ultimate source of our power, creativity, and life. I believe this separation is a temporary condition and that we have the power to "come home" when we choose, to return to our awareness of the divine, to the knowledge of our souls and Spirit. I believe this is the message of all great spiritual teachers throughout all time. It is a universal message and remains the same, no matter the time, culture, or tradition. In the Gospel according to Luke, it is written that Jesus taught the parable of the lost son, the prodigal son who realizes the error of his ways and comes home to his father. (Luke 15: 20 – 24, New International Version.) Though in the parable, the emphasis is on the son who comes home, I think of it as the parable of the "forgiving Father," for it exemplifies the nature of God, which sees the perfection of each soul no matter what the circumstances and experiences only love.

> *While he was still a long way off, his father saw him and was filled with compassion for him; he ran to his son, threw his arms around him and kissed him. The son said to him, "Father, I have sinned against heaven and against you. I am no longer worthy to be called your son." But the father said to his servants, "Quick! Bring the best robe and put it on him. Put a ring on his finger and sandals on his feet. Bring the fattened calf and kill it. Let's have a feast and celebrate. For this son of mine was dead and is alive again; he was lost and is found." So they began to celebrate.*

It is natural for fathers and mothers to rejoice when their children come home. Homecoming celebrations are repeated worldwide on many occasions and in many circumstances. When there is great loving and when times of separation come to an end, we all celebrate the homecoming of our loved ones. Does it not follow that when we, who are the children of God, find our way home to the Father, there will be rejoicing beyond anything imaginable by our human consciousness? But that is closer to the end of the story. This story begins when a certain man had two sons.

> *The younger son said to his father, "Father, give me my share of the estate." So he divided his property between them. Not long after that, the younger son got together all he had, set off for a distant country and there squandered his wealth in wild living.*

I look upon myself as someone very much like the prodigal son. I "left home" long ago and have wandered the lands of the emotions, mind, imagination, and materiality for a long time. The lands of Spirit, soul, and God—my true home—became dim and nearly forgotten. I cannot tell you exactly what caused me, in this lifetime, to hear the call of my Father, *"When are you coming home?"* I only know that I did. Perhaps there is a timing that exists outside our conscious awareness. Perhaps God calls to each and every one of His sons and daughters, and perhaps we all hear and then, in our own special timing, choose when and how we answer.

The awakening of my soul has been a gradual process. It has involved many experiences, teachers, mistakes, highs, and lows. The awakening of my soul has taught me about the soul, about its qualities and strengths, about its journey, and about its eternal nature.

When I was a young man and went off to college, I left the physical home I had known with my parents, brother, and sisters. I left the security of that home, my community, friends, emotional support, and a kind of intrinsic caring and loving I had known since childhood. I moved from a small rural town to a bigger city. I went to a larger school. Some normal insecurities appeared. I did my best to conceal them with bravado (which might also be called ego).

To allay my feelings of separation and insecurity, I tried to win the approval of potential new friends, teachers— whoever was around. I spent a lot of time trying to please other people, thinking that would bring me security in the world. And I was actually pretty skilled at it and had some minor social successes as a result, but after a while, I sensed I was missing the things that I really wanted in my life.

I was missing true loving and genuine caring. I was worshiping the god of opinion way too much. I was too concerned about what "they" said and what "they" thought.

I kept modifying or changing my responses to please others. And gradually, I lost the sense of who I was, the boy I had been in the context of my family and community. I knew that my body was doing certain things and my emotions had some feelings about those things. My mind had a lot of negative thoughts about myself, the people around me, and the world in general because I didn't like what I was doing or what was happening around me.

In school, I studied, not to learn, but to get a good grade on the test. I didn't pay any attention to what I actually thought or felt about a subject. I just tried to memorize what I believed the teacher wanted to hear on the test. I was busy sacrificing my integrity and feeling uncomfortable about it.

I remember wanting rather desperately to be in with a certain group of my peers. I tried to say what they would say, and do what they would do, and answer what they would answer, so they would accept me and like me and let me be one of them. But unbeknownst to me, they didn't want another one just like themselves; they wanted somebody different. So they didn't choose me. In looking back, I can see how fortunate I was, but at the time I just thought the world was against me. I was busy judging myself, them, the system, and everything around me.

I was so busy judging that I was losing track of who was doing the judging. Where was "I"? Where was that part of me that was the essence?

I found out that when I tried so hard to please others, it became easier and easier to lie. Someone would mention something that I had told another person, and I would think (judge) that the person talking to me now didn't like my point of view, so I would deny what I had said and change my story. I would say what I thought this new person wanted to hear. And then when the next person came along and mentioned that they had heard what I had said—if I thought they disapproved—I'd tell yet another story. In time, I knew this wasn't working well at all. I was confused and upset most of the time, and the result of all my "people-pleasing" behavior was that no one liked me very much. Some people tolerated me, but it didn't seem like I was making the kind of friends I wanted, nor living the kind of life I wanted.

I seemed to have lost the sense of my own center that I'd experienced at home when I was younger. Now I seemed to be almost "outside myself" much of the time. I was more concerned with what other people believed and thought than with what I did. The sense of belonging was gone. I felt alone and separated whether I was with the people who had become so important to me, or whether I was by myself. I was fast becoming miserable. Something had to change.

I decided I'd watch my life for about six months and see if I could simply observe what was happening. I'd try to be objective about myself, and see if some kind of objective neutrality might bring about insight and change. I began to watch my own behavior with more honesty. I began to admit to myself when I was lying, when I was changing my stories in order to please others. I began to question myself about why I was behaving these ways. In time I realized I was afraid that if I stood up for something—if I expressed a firm point of view and didn't back off at the first sign of disapproval—I would not be able to support myself emotionally. I was afraid I'd look weak or stupid or uneducated or any number of other things I judged as being bad or wrong.

With this realization came the awakening of a voice deep inside of me that admonished me to speak my truth, whatever my truth was at any given time. I recognized the rightness of that admonition to speak the truth, even though it was pretty frightening to me at the time. Who within me stood up for truth? I sensed my soul awakening, though I had no words for it. I knew this was the right path, though I did not know where it might lead me.

Somewhere deep within, I could sense God's presence and could hear that silent question, *"When are you coming home? When will you recognize you are spirit, you are soul, you are a rightful heir to the kingdom of heaven?"*

I resolved that, no matter how popular or unpopular it would be, I would say what seemed correct to me. I would say what I believed to be true. I decided that I wouldn't seek to speak out just to hear myself talk, but if asked or if it seemed important, I would say the truth. For many, many weeks after I came to this decision and decided to implement this change, I had very little to say to anybody. My mind, for once, became very quiet. I was so practiced at discovering what other people thought and then saying what I thought they wanted to hear that it took me some time to discover what I thought. Now, when I didn't know what I thought or felt about something, I consciously chose to stay quiet.

As I spent more time being quiet, I found that my mind became still. Then my emotions seemed to settle down because I didn't have to be concerned about what others thought. Then my body stopped aching and hurting. And a small voice from deep inside me rewarded my new behavior with the thought, "Now you're getting smart."

There was still much separation within me. I cannot say that I knew myself in any significant way. I still did not know there was a spark of God that lived within me and that it would guide me if I would listen, would comfort me if I would allow it, and would provide the connection and the sense of belonging I was looking for. These things were still hidden, but they were beginning to be revealed.

As time passed, I sought out people who had more knowledge than I, who seemed wiser, who seemed to have an experience that I was after, and from whom I could learn. My quest became to know myself. My quest was to find out who I was, to discover who it was who said "my body feels this" or "my feelings are these" or "my thoughts are unclear"—and to find out who said, "Tell the truth. Now you're getting smart." Who claimed "*my* body," "*my* feelings," "*my* thoughts"? I was not yet thinking about soul, but the sense and the awareness of there being something beyond my physical form was becoming clearer.

In the Bible, the story of the lost or prodigal son takes only a few paragraphs. And the narrative is told mostly from the point of view of the father and the good son. There is not much in the story about the prodigal son's point of view. One might imagine that the process of the prodigal son—looked at from the prodigal son's point of view—would be a complex and interesting one. But the story as we know it says:

After he spent everything, there was a severe famine in that whole country and he began to be in need.

Need is not always a physical need. In my late teens and early twenties, one difficulty I had was my attitude toward my life. This is not an uncommon problem, particularly in our Western culture where so much is given to us. We have such abundance that we often come to expect it. Perhaps the prodigal son experienced this, too. The story implies that he had once been wealthy and experienced abundance. Sometimes, when we have a lot, we begin to think it is our due, that we are owed a certain level of comfort and convenience. Nothing, however, could be further from the truth. Of course, this doesn't stop us from projecting our own ego point of view out to the universe and God and demanding to be provided with goods and services to our heart's content. One need I had was for a change of attitude and more gratitude for what I did have. In time, I experienced that moving toward greater gratitude moved me closer to my spiritual home. It was part of my journey and of my soul's awakening.

IN THE MANY WAYS WE CAN FEEL SEPARATE, it is often challenging to realize there is a different option, different from defending our points of view, different from worrying so much what others will think about us. Perhaps the states of separation are temporary, but often they run together, making it difficult to listen to a quieter voice, a voice of wisdom.

Take a moment now and consider that beyond your body, mind, and emotions, there is something more enduring, something greater.

Have you sensed it? Have you ever wondered about it? Do you ever feel a kind of yearning for "home" without even knowing what that is or how it might be different from your present experience? Have you ever heard an echo of a whisper inside you that might be saying, "When are you coming home?" What if your life here on Earth is only part of your story? What if there is more?

Consider trying on an attitude of openness. Now, think about what your attitude would be if you knew there is a place already prepared for you, a place that is your rightful home. It is a place kept safe and sacred for you until you are ready to accept that it exists and are ready to move toward it.

You know you'll be welcomed there by the most loving being you can imagine. Wouldn't your attitude include elements of gratitude, enthusiasm, peace, and loving? Wouldn't you be so grateful to know you are coming home?

If you would practice Soul Transcendence, you might begin by practicing gratitude. Try it for an hour or a day or a week. Be creative. Try it on simple things. Try it in areas where you wouldn't normally experience gratitude. And when life seems too difficult or too sad or too hurtful, lift your perspective and ask your soul to show you how you can use your experiences to learn to be grateful, to let go of judgments, and to expand your loving.

To know more of the soul, look with the eyes and hear with the ears of gratitude.

CHAPTER TWO

FINDING GOD IN LIFE'S MUD HOLE

TWO

One day, when I had awakened more fully to my soul and to its timelessness and eternal nature, I was complaining to myself about my lot in life and placing a subtle—or maybe not so subtle—demand on God and Spirit to provide me with something better. The memories of another time and place began to take shape inside my mind. With these memories came questions of how I could be remembering something from another time and place. Nevertheless, I held steady with my experience and, as I did so, it became evident to me that the soul, which is my essence, my individualized spark of God, had had many other experiences at other times and in other places.

It seems that this particular earthly experience is but one of many. There have been a myriad of others. Through my soul, there is a connection within me to all the experiences this soul has ever had, and there are times when this present-day embodiment (me) experiences the memories of other times and places. It's not so very different from remembering something from your childhood; it just goes a little bit further back in time. This kind of "far memory" doesn't happen all the time, nor does it happen upon demand. Generally, it happens when there is a specific reason for it. Spirit seems to be efficient and ecological in its approach to all things. Nothing is wasted. If there is no use for memory (far or near), experience, or awareness, it simply does not occur. If there is use, it is presented generously.

This particular far memory seemed at first to be a little like a dream, but the *experience* I had as the memory came to me was not like a dream at all. It was more like a call to awakening or a kick in the pants. The memory was of a time (not too far in the past, though not in this life) when I was learning a great lesson about priorities, attachment, and detachment. I had been on what you might call a spiritual path, consciously studying Spirit and God, and I also had money and privilege, at least at the beginning.

At some point, all the success that had been part of my outer life began to fall away. Things went badly for me in business. Then I lost my business. I lost money. Friends left me. My loved ones left me. My home was taken from me. It was quite like the trials of Job in the Bible, except that Job seemed aware that God had a part in what was happening. I wasn't so sure. Job was clear that he was being plagued by the devil. I didn't have that kind of awareness. There wasn't any devil I could identify. There was just a progression of disastrous events. All I knew was that everything was falling away from me, and before very long, I ended up with nothing left but myself. This was indeed "being in need," as is said of the prodigal son. I had lost my home. My friends got tired of lending me money and providing me places to stay. Eventually, I was reduced to living on the streets. I had no money. I couldn't seem to get any kind of job. I'd go days without having anything to eat. Sometimes I'd fight the street dogs for scraps of food. That's pretty low, particularly when I lost out to them as many times as I did. As time went on, even my clothes began to disintegrate and fall off me. I had only a few shreds of clothing left, not enough to keep me warm at night.

One night, I came upon a mud hole and, in an effort at survival, realized that if I smeared mud on my body, the mud would dry and provide some barrier to the cold air. I tried it, and it did, indeed, keep me warmer than before. In the daytime, however, I had to find someplace to get the mud off so that I wouldn't bake in it. So, a lot of my time was taken up in finding a mud hole for the nighttime and then finding a place to clean the mud off for the daytime.

This went on for quite a long time. And in this process, I learned a lot about breathing in and breathing out. Spending most of my time taking care of simple survival taught me a lot. I didn't have time to think about or care about many things beyond my basic survival. And in that focus, I began to think more and more about God. I began to think more about myself as a part of God. I began to think about the earlier times, when I was abundant, when I was concerned about money, appearances, friends, and image. I began to see that all those things were choices. I had chosen to be concerned about those things. Now, they seemed superfluous to my real self.

I was beginning to see that my self was my self, even without friends, money, house, car, or spouse. After all that had happened to me, after all that I'd had and all that had been taken away, I was still my self. And God was still God.

That was something to contemplate. I began to suspect, like Job, that perhaps God did have a hand in all of this. I wondered, was there a purpose to this? Was I in the mud hole to learn? I decided that, on the off chance that God was a part of my experience, I would not curse God in my ignorance. And in my ignorance, I would not curse other people. I would not blame. I would not speculate as to why this was happening to me and not to other people who had so much more. I would not compare my experience with theirs. I was beginning to realize that my experience was perfectly designed for me and that I could, perhaps, learn from it. And so I learned as best I could.

I learned that, if this was the worst that could befall me, I could survive it. I learned that my happiness was not dependent on things in this world. I learned that I always, minute to minute, had a choice of whether to be happy or not. I began to know that this experience would not break me. I would not fall apart. I would not cease to exist. I experienced myself as being resourceful, diligent, hopeful, caring, and creative. These are good qualities. These are the things that sustained me. I was as low as I could go in terms of this physical world. And one thing I found out was that, after being down and out, so to speak, everything else is a step up. I was lying flat on my back, flattened by circumstances, so everything from that point on was truly looking up.

As I began to see how strong I was, I began to experience myself not as an outcast from society, but as part of a greater reality. The world—with its usual concerns of family, friends, home, and work—had essentially ceased to exist for me. All those usual reference points and points of identification were gone. I was outside of all that. If I was not to go mad and die in the despair of my situation, I had to find out what I was still a part of. I had to find out what I was inside of. And what I found was God. I found a kind of essential beingness. I found that in my breath—in my breathing in and out—I had an identity. I was part of something. I was part of myself.

I was part of God. As long as I had breath, that identity could not be taken from me.

In time, as an essential part of my breathing in and out, I began to breathe the name of God. I began to say the name of God over and over and over, wherever I was, whatever I was doing. I found that it had a kind of sustaining power. It connected me to something that was completely other than my present experience. Some nights, I curled up with stray animals, and they gave me warmth. I would lie there, close to the animals, and say the name of God, over and over. I was warm and I was safe and I was alive.

Finally, I gave up expecting things to change. I gave up wanting to "get back on my feet." I gave up having an opinion about what was happening. Inside of myself, I said, "I don't know how long this is going to go on. I don't know how long I will be here. But if it's a long time, I guess that's okay, because I don't know that I have any choice right now." And from deep within myself, I experienced a certainty that I had endured what was given to me to endure. I realized that I had changed in some very profound ways. I knew the world would never be the same for me, that I would always have another reference point, that the glamour of the world would never entice me as it had. But I didn't think about there being a spiritual home to which I could go and be received with total and unconditional loving. I didn't realize that God might have been calling me home. But I did learn very important lessons in that life, and within a very short period of time, things began to change. People who had forsaken me sought me out and provided food, clothing, and shelter. Money that had been owed to me was paid. Things that had been taken from me were returned.

As I received the things that were returned to me, I realized how unimportant they were. I could hardly believe I had ever cared about these things. I gave them away. As moneys owed were paid to me, I gave them away. I did move to a better situation and provided myself with adequate food, clothing, and a physical home, but I didn't keep excess. I gave much to those who had a greater need than I.

As my fortunes returned, and as things were, indeed, "looking up," I realized that it was when I was saying the name of God over and over and over that I had felt the happiest. I had felt the most connected to a greater reality that exists beyond all the material things of this world. I realized that, even if I had food and clothing, I could still say the name of God. It was nice to say the name of God over and over and over in a clean, comfortable environment. But it was not so very different from saying the name of God over and over while feeling safe and warm among the animals.

I had learned that regardless of the outer situation, God is. I had learned that when I was aware of God, when I was aware of divinity being present, I was in touch with my soul, which is the part of God individualized within me, within you, within each of us.

That's what I learned in the mud hole. I learned I had an enduring and eternal connection with God and my soul, and that it is more valuable than anything in this world. I learned to live from the center of my soul. I learned that success in this world and failure in this world are as nothing when compared to the soul.

THE STORY PAINTS A PICTURE OF EXTREME
LOSS *leading to profound triumphs of inner discovery.
Have you ever lost something you felt was so important you
wondered if you could live without it? How did you regain
your sense of self, your experience of wholeness? What did
you learn about the thing you lost? Was it as important as
you first thought? What did you learn about yourself—and
how you outlasted or overcame this challenge?*

*John-Roger talks about how focusing on his breath took
him through very challenging times. Breath is a gift from
God—a simple and sure way to be in touch with Spirit
and soul.*

*Yet breathing is something we take for granted because we
do it all day and all night, every day and every night. We
don't have to think about it. It goes on, in the background,
steady and constant. Much like Spirit. Much like God.*

It's usually only when we lose our breath that we notice it. We notice it when we dive too deep in the lake and have trouble getting to the surface fast enough. We notice it if we get short of breath from too much exertion or perhaps when in high altitude. We notice it if we are ill and having trouble breathing. But most of the time, we just breathe.

Breathing—with conscious awareness that your breath is a gift from God—is one way to experience your soul's presence. When you breathe consciously—deeply, peacefully, and fully—you can touch the simplicity of your soul's divine nature. It is a wonderful way to experience all is well on a very fundamental level.

Try this:
Inhale to the count of four—and exhale to the count of four.
Pause, and wait for God to breathe you.
Wait for your soul to take your next breath.
Then breathe in to the count of four—and out to the count of four.

Relax. Be quiet.
Wait for God to breathe you.
Repeat this for several minutes.
Place your awareness on what breathes you when you
relax, and wait for your breath to come to you. Place your
awareness on what lies beyond your conscious control.
How are you feeling now?

Soul Transcendence is the practice of awareness: awareness of
yourself, awareness of your soul, awareness of God. Beyond
all the activities of this life, beyond successes and failures,
beyond relationships, beyond acquisitions, there is the soul.
It is what outlasts all the rest of it. The soul is what you
can count on. It is the vehicle for your expression here.
When you were born to this physical earth, the soul was
your vehicle, and it will be your vehicle when you leave
this earth plane.

If you would practice Soul Transcendence, get to know your
soul and discover what it finds important and worthwhile.
Here's a clue: it may not be a new car or a bigger house or

more money. And it's probably not whether you are short or tall, thin or chubby, have straight or curly hair, or whether you can run a marathon in less than three hours. Here's another clue: ask what inside of you remains steady through all of the ups and downs, the losses and gains of life.

CHAPTER THREE

CHOOSING BEYOND SEPARATION

THREE

The story of the prodigal son intrigues me. It doesn't reveal anything about the family and the two brothers before the younger brother left home. But there must have been something in the home that was loving and safe because, in time, even though he had fallen on hard times, the "lost son" thought:

> "I will set out and go back to my father and say to him:
> 'Father I have sinned against heaven and against you.
> I am no longer worthy to be called your son; make me
> like one of your hired men.' So he got up and went to
> his father."

Even though he had made mistakes and been lost to his father for a long time, he knew he could return to his father's house.

I grew up in a home that provided me with a foundation of loving and support. It wasn't a perfect home, but there were aspects about it that were perfect. I grew up with three sisters, a brother, my mom and dad. I was a pretty active and curious kid. I had a lot of questions when

I was young. Why could my brother sometimes get away with some things and I couldn't? Why did the girls get special things? What were relationships about? Why did we love? Why did we hate? What made us happy or sad? Why did we get angry? Why did each of us respond differently?

As I got older, I wondered why some people seemed to have a happy, positive outlook on life while others were so unhappy. I wondered why some people were successful and some were not and why success came in so many different guises. Some people didn't seem to have material wealth but were wealthy in other ways—such as loving, happiness, family, faith, and gratitude. Others seemed to have everything going for them but weren't particularly happy, always wanting more or wanting something different.

From a place of curiosity, I observed my family and how they related to one another and to me. They taught me a lot. One time when my sister was young, she didn't receive an invitation to the high school prom from the boy she wanted to go with. She was feeling terrible. She was unhappy and depressed and felt that her world had just crashed in on her, and she felt like our mother wasn't being properly sympathetic. Mother was just going on with life as usual, and her words of wisdom to my sister were, "Don't worry, honey, you can't stay sad forever. In a little while, you'll start to feel better." I watched, and it was true. My sister felt miserable for a while longer, and then she didn't. Another boy asked her out. Things changed. She found other interests, other things that were valuable to her, and life became good again in her eyes. I looked at the whole process she went through, and I wondered what that was all about. Did she have to feel bad to begin with? Since she eventually felt good again, could she have felt good all along? What made the difference?

One thing I noticed was that when people—me, my sister, my parents—felt bad, they created a sense of separation. When I was angry with my brother, I wanted him to stay away, to leave me alone. I pulled away and went off by myself. The same thing happened when my sister or anyone else was feeling bad; they cut themselves off from everybody else.

My mother would say to my sister, "Don't worry, honey, in a little while you'll start to feel better." I wondered if it was her way of letting my sister know that in her unhappiness, she was separating herself, but that it was temporary and she would move back into a sense of connection before too long. Have you ever noticed that you can be feeling really bad, unhappy, like no one cares about you, and then someone comes up to you and gives you a compliment or gives you a hug and says, "I sure do love you," and all of a sudden, your unhappiness just vanishes? All of a sudden, people are good again and you feel good about yourself and everything seems to be just fine. What happened? Probably, you moved from separation to connection or to a feeling of oneness. That shift is powerful. It reflects a choice. At any moment, we can choose separation or we can choose connection. Later on I realized that as powerful as this choice is on the physical level, it is much more powerful on the spiritual level.

Babies and very young children are masters at choosing connection and oneness. Given a choice, they will almost always choose connection and, in their choosing, they often express a quality of innocence that I have since recognized as being a quality of the soul. The soul is a very simple thing. It is God's gift to us of Himself, a gift of awareness, consciousness, of life itself. It is the part of us that most purely belongs to God. When we have awareness of the soul, we have awareness of God and our belonging with God. And we are happy in that. The soul knows the experience of connection. A child, when born to this world, wants to experience himself or herself as belonging to his family. His soul knows the joy and loving that come from connection with God. He seeks to recreate that essential connection here on Earth. A child wants to be accepted and loved.

There is an innocence in how little children relate to their environment, in the way they ask for the love they need, in the ways they seek to belong. As children become a little older some of that innocence is often lost. Achievement becomes important. They learn to bargain. The idea of rewards and punishments makes an impression. That simple state of being is replaced by the imperative to do, to achieve, and to compete. The soul steps back as these other qualities of the mind, body, and emotions assert themselves. Often by nine or ten years old—and certainly by adolescence—a child is concerned with the goals his parents have for him and the ones he has for himself. He's concerned about how he measures up against his siblings and peers, what is and is not acceptable to his friends, about scholastic achievements, society's expectations, and many other factors.

The simplicity and the innocence that is the soul becomes somewhat overpowered by the demands of the world. When dad criticizes you, it's hard to remember that you are precious and perfect in God's eyes. When your friends think you're a nerd for wanting to go with your family on a camping trip, it's hard to connect to the truth inside of you or to recognize its value. When your mom withdraws her love and becomes angry and cold, it's hard to imagine that you might still be a good person. And it's almost impossible not to believe that, if you could just mold your thoughts, beliefs, feelings, and body to a form that would please those all-important and powerful people around you, you would belong. And you would be safe. And you would be whole. That is the promise our families, our culture, and our world seem to hold out to us. But there is another promise, a spiritual promise made to us by God, that we are already loved and valued for who we are, not for what we do or say, not for how we look, not for our jobs, and not for whether or not we agree with those around us. The spiritual promise is that we are all heirs to the kingdom of God because we are the sons and daughters of God. And our souls are our beacon to guide us home to that safe haven, no matter how difficult we have made our journey.

When I was a kid, I had a best friend with whom I shared a lot. He was a little older than I was and a little bigger. But sometimes I had a smarter mouth. And sometimes—as little boys will do—we'd get in a disagreement of some kind. I'd say something that would upset him and he'd hit me. If I hit him back, he'd just "kill" me (and you know how bad that can hurt). Sometimes when he hit me, it really upset and hurt me. But sometimes, I'd see it from a perspective that would make it so funny that I'd start laughing. He'd get even angrier and hit me again. I'd laugh more, and he'd hit more. It would get funnier and funnier, and the more I'd laugh, the more he would hit me. But it never hurt.

As I was laughing, I'd taunt him, "I don't think you can hit me hard enough to hurt me." So of course, he'd try harder. And then I'd say, "Wait until my folks see all these bruises." He'd say, "You won't tell, will you?" because his mom and my mom talked to each other. I'd say, "Probably, I will." And that would be even more hilarious, so I'd laugh harder. He'd be so frustrated, but eventually, he'd realize that he couldn't hit me hard enough to hurt me. And I'd realize he couldn't hurt me because I was disregarding what he was doing and maintaining a sense of my own center inside. What was actually happening—though I didn't have the words for it then—was that I was in touch with a greater part of myself that knew the things of this world could not touch it. I was in touch with something greater than my physical body (which was getting beaten), greater than my imagination (which could have seen myself being badly hurt), greater than my emotions (which could have felt my best friend hated and rejected me), and greater than my mind (which could have judged what a terrible situation this was and what a terrible life I was having). I was in touch with something beyond all of that, which saw two boys battling each other for identity and for power. Nothing to be concerned about. Nothing to get upset about. Souls gaining experience. That's all, though I couldn't have told you that at the time. At the time, I just knew that something happening in this world that was supposed to make me unhappy and disturbed didn't necessarily have to do that. I could find a different perspective and maintain a happy point of view.

This slightly transcendent experience by way of laughter was a mini-experience of my soul and its power, though I certainly didn't have that perspective when I was a child. What I was discovering, though, was that any time I got hit, I had an immediate choice. I could go with the pain and the suffering of the situation which might have been reflected in thoughts, such as, "He's bigger than I am. I can't do anything about this. He always picks on me. This hurts. This is terrible." The other choice—the one I took—was one of humor, of seeing the reality that he was not going to hurt me, indeed, could not hurt me unless I gave him that power over me. This kind of choice speaks to the duality of the human condition. We have the choice, moment to moment, to choose the negative point of view or choose a more positive, uplifting, life-affirming point of view.

Positive and negative. Two extremes. Two poles of a battery. When positive and negative are in a relationship to one another, they supply an energy. They supply a charge. I think that in human beings, it is the proximity of both the positive and the negative and their relationship that creates a kind of charge, a tension that propels us through our life and through our experiences.

Did I always laugh when my best friend hit me? No, sometimes I responded with anger, and sometimes I hit back. Sometimes I felt hurt or betrayed. But sometimes, there would be that spontaneous presence—something I didn't have a word for—that would provide perfect protection from harm and hurt. I remembered this experience. During times when I could not or would not find that presence within me, it nonetheless remained in my memory as a reference point. Similarly, the prodigal son, when his fortunes in the world were failing and times were difficult, might have had a reference point of being safe in his father's house, and he might have remembered that there was a place within him that was safe from harm and hurt, no matter what the outer circumstances were.

WHAT ARE YOUR REFERENCE POINTS FOR CHOOSING ONENESS *when in the experience of separation? At a time when you overcame separation, what helped you reach out—to another, or inside yourself—for more oneness? What did you discover about yourself?*

Innocence is a quality of the soul. There is an innocence in being available to Spirit because you suspend your doubt and skepticism and allow the marvelous "what if?" to entice you into new experiences and discoveries. Children let their imaginations conjure up wonderful adventures and explorations. You can, too, when you let yourself experience the freedom of innocence.

If you want to experience Soul Transcendence, let yourself explore "what if?" from a place of innocence and wonderment. What if you do have the power to choose light over darkness? What if you have the power to choose connection and oneness over separation and loneliness? To look for the blessings in every moment? To love yourself no matter what?

Next time life presents a challenge to you and you find yourself feeling separate, lonely, angry, resentful, or hurt—stop and allow yourself to ask, "What if I have another choice?" Let yourself see through the eyes of a child. See how you can reach out through and past your negative experience to what you really want—love, comfort, understanding, belonging. Realize that even if no one else is there to give you those things, you can give them to yourself. You can reach inside to a place of loving and positive focus, making yourself more available to your soul and the wholeness you seek.

As you practice choosing the positive, you are practicing Soul Transcendence.

CHAPTER FOUR

COMING TO MY SENSES,
FINDING NEW SENSES

FOUR

The story of the prodigal son moves swiftly over the time between his leaving home and his decision to return home. I have often wondered about all the experiences he may have had before he "came to his senses" and decided to find his way home. Surely, it is a parable and, as such, simply the essence of the complete story. How much did it take for him to come to his senses?

There have been several incidents in my life when I walked very close to physical death. There were illnesses, accidents, and all sorts of strange situations. The catastrophes always seemed to disperse before anything happened that was too damaging. But through it all, I kept breathing in and breathing out. I knew what I was doing and that my prime directive through these times was to keep breathing. Perhaps the great learning that had been mine from my previous life in the mud hole was still with me on some level. Perhaps I intuitively knew that my breath was my connection to Spirit and to God.

When I was young, swimming in a lake, I developed a cramp that was so severe I had great difficulty staying on top of the water, much less swimming toward shore. I went down and came up, went down and came up, four or five times. On about the fifth trip up for air, I realized that I really might drown. The intensity of that realization and the desire for life and for my next breath moved my consciousness in a way it had never moved before. I broke the cramp and found myself moving through the water so dynamically, it was almost as if the shore reached out and pulled me up. I recognized the tremendous force of life within me and my tremendous desire to continue with my life. It was a powerful lesson in awareness and in the sacredness of life, which I have never forgotten.

Then, during my young adulthood, I had two major surgeries. Both times during the surgeries, I realized that I was watching the surgery take place from a level entirely different from the physical. On the physical level, I was unconscious and sedated with anesthetics. On another level, I could see and I could hear, and I was totally aware of what was happening—though not with my physical senses. During my first surgery, I realized I was very detached from the physical events, though completely aware of them. And more than that, the consciousness I was experiencing was neutral, benevolent, peaceful, and loving. It was as though I was having a direct experience of some greater reality—a greater reality of myself, of life, of Spirit. I felt more alive than I ever had, even when I nearly drowned as a child. In that moment, "sacredness of life" took on an entirely new meaning. Suddenly, there was *more* than I had ever considered. More awareness, more possibilities, more life force. There were energy patterns present that I had never perceived before. Sometimes the energy seemed like smoke being blown in a glass. Sometimes it was brighter than that, shimmering, alive. Sometimes there was a luminescence, a brilliance, a sense of space and expansion and clarity. It was as though it was all being illuminated from within. And throughout it all, there was a sense of peace—as though I was perfectly protected and safe. I felt tremendous joy. I was experiencing a sense of bliss beyond anything I had ever imagined. I felt more real than I ever had before. *This* was the reality that I wanted to experience all the time. *This* was the consciousness I wanted to be— totally, continually, in every way. *This* was the me I wanted to be—consciously—with 100-percent awareness. *This* was what I wanted to be present always.

As all of this was unfolding, I knew I was not dreaming because these experiences were much too "solid," too real. I knew exactly what was happening physically, but it was not my only level of knowing. There was a quality of multidimensional awareness: I was aware of both my physical body and its experience and, also, this other experience of simultaneously being on another plane and living a different reality. I found I could see a bigger picture than was normal or usual for me. I knew that if I were experiencing the surgery from a purely physical point of view, I would be frightened, concerned, worried, controlling, and for me, that would be constricting. What I was actually experiencing was understanding, hope, optimism, and loving, which included feeling love toward myself, the doctors, nurses, everyone. There was a sense of expansion unlike anything I had ever known. This was fantastic. This was wonderful.

Even upon awakening from the anesthetic, I thought how terrific it would be to experience this kind of positive awareness at all times. Not just in times of emergency, but all the time. Deep inside of me, I became aware that this was more important to me than anything else had ever been. To have that loving, peaceful feeling inside, no matter what was happening on the physical level, I knew I could (and would) sacrifice everything I had known in the world. To have that loving consciousness entirely present, I was willing to let go of my ego demands, my entrenched positions of personality, my opinions and points of view. I wanted this sense of expanded consciousness so badly that I was willing to give up everything if I could just be *that* and know *that* every day. To have that loving, joyous feeling, to have that complete attunement, to know that oneness that never ends—that would be worth everything.

I was experiencing a glimpse of the spiritual promise, the awareness that I was loved by Spirit and by God and that I was safe, no matter the outcome of the surgery.

The experience of a higher, greater reality was even stronger during and after the second surgery. During the time I was anesthetized and unconscious from a physical point of view, I was very conscious of a great spiritual Light encompassing both my physical body and my greater consciousness. I was aware of other levels of existence and reality. Beings of Light—angels if you will—were all around me. It was a tremendously humbling experience to become aware of these great and beautiful beings of Light and Spirit and of the scope of this greater reality. Why me? Why was I being allowed to see and experience this? From my finite and imperfect human consciousness, this made no sense. Could it be that there was a greater consciousness available, within which this did make sense? I was willing to believe in that possibility. I opened up to innocence. And it was as if the angels and beings of Light burst forth and all things became new to me. I heard joyous hallelujahs from all around and felt tremendous patterns of energy sweep through me, tremendous heat, tremendous joy. I felt a great spiritual consciousness touch to me and felt myself being lifted into a consciousness greater than any consciousness I expressed on the physical level. I was willing to let the ego be sacrificed to discover my true self, my greater self, my soul.

Later, I realized this awakening and expansion into Spirit is the heritage of every soul. Every soul, in its own timing, will awaken to the greater Spirit and return to its home.

After the surgery was over, I was quite reluctant to return to the physical world. I liked what I had experienced of the other dimension so much better. There was so much promise there of joy, fulfillment, and peace. But there is a wisdom in each individual soul that knows the correct path to be taken in its journey home to God. My soul knew there was more for me to learn and to do on the physical plane called Earth.

And so I recovered from the surgeries and went on with my life, and for a time, things seemed pretty much as they had been before. But now when things in my life were difficult or challenging, I was more successful in moving my con-sciousness to the peaceful neutrality and loving I had experienced during the surgeries. I began to see more consistently through the eyes of loving and compassion. This made it easier to do things in a way that supported what was best for everyone, not necessarily what I wanted from my own personal perspective. My behavior changed. I became more understanding, kinder, able to see points of view other than my own. I listened to people with greater empathy. My experience during the surgeries of all things being "in the Light" and the safety and security I had experienced in that higher consciousness began to express into the physical world. No matter what was happening, I could see it as being part of a greater whole, part of the highest good, part of the process of learning and growing. I began to think of these changes as a change of consciousness because I was behaving so very differently in my life. In a way, it felt like I was coming to my senses.

In the story of the prodigal son, it says:

> *When he came to his senses, he said, "How many of my father's hired men have food to spare, and here I am starving to death. I will set out and go back to my father and say to him: "Father, I have sinned against heaven and against you. I am no longer worthy to be called your son; make me like one of your hired men." So he got up and went to his father. But while he was still a long way off, his father saw him and was filled with compassion for him; he ran to his son, threw his arms around him and kissed him.*

Perhaps "coming to my senses" had been precipitated by the surgeries. Certainly coming to my senses had some landmark moments, but the overall process was a gradual one. It was happening moment to moment, day by day. In the story of the prodigal son, we are told of one moment when he realized he didn't have to live separately from his father and family but could go home. I'd guess that, like mine, the process of coming to his senses was more gradual than the story tells. And perhaps the most important part of the story is the father's compassion for his son because it exemplifies the spirit of God manifested through this man. It exemplifies the soul's oneness with God—individualized as the son and yet of the same essence as the Father.

HAVE YOU HAD A TIME *when something called you to come to your senses to experience life in the context of a bigger picture? How did this change your sense of yourself?*

Have you been touched deeply by someone's kindness? What did it awaken in you?

Kindness and compassion are qualities of the soul you can practice anytime, anywhere. You don't have to be rich. You don't have to be smart. You don't have to have all the answers. Kindness and compassion are like a breath of fresh air. We know that breath is a universal gift from God, available to all equally. Kindness and compassion are gifts you can give yourself and others without qualification.

When you are unhappy or dissatisfied with something you have done (or have not done), you have the perfect opportunity to practice kindness and compassion. When you find yourself unhappy or upset with what someone else has done (or not done), you have another perfect opportunity to practice kindness and compassion.

Here's a way you can do it: When you find yourself upset or annoyed, stop and take a breath. Just breathe. Gradually you come present. Then focus on expanding your consciousness to encompass a bigger perspective than the one you are seeing. That's a way to get to compassion. Maybe you try seeing the situation from the other person's point of view. Think of how they might be feeling or what they may be dealing with. Maybe you look ahead in time and ask yourself if the situation will be important enough to matter in five years—or ten. You may check to see if your reaction is from your ego and if your ego is important enough to risk hurting yourself or another. You can look at the situation impersonally, as if it were happening to someone else. Or take yourself out of it and pretend you are seeing from the top of a mountain.

These are some simple ways you can expand your consciousness. Once you have expanded your consciousness and have seen the situation from a higher perspective, it's likely you will begin to experience compassion—for yourself and for others.

Kindness, then, is compassion put into action. Kindness is helping someone up when they have fallen. Kindness is encouraging someone who is having a hard time. Kindness sometimes can be just smiling at someone as you walk by, holding the door for someone even if you have to wait a few seconds, picking up what someone drops, rubbing someone's shoulders, or returning a phone call from someone who loves you.

As kindness comes in infinite forms, there is no shortage of creative opportunity for expressing it. Kindness can be enormously fun to practice because it often catches people by surprise. You can see their faces slowly melt into a smile or break out into a grin.

If you want to practice Soul Transcendence, practice adopting a higher perspective; practice kindness and compassion.

CHAPTER FIVE

LEARNING TO BE THE STUDENT

F I V E

O ne day, while I was still in college—before the surgeries and that level of my spiritual awakening—I had
attended the lecture of a man who was a pioneer in what
today we would call a *holistic* approach to healing, though I
don't believe the word holistic was part of our vocabulary in
the 1950's. As a psychology student at the time, I was accustomed to hearing lots of theories, but I rarely could verify
the information I received because it all remained quite the-
oretical. But this man departed from theory. He had trained
in traditional healing methods (both physical and psycholog-
ical), but he also carried a strong belief in the ability of the
body, in conjunction with the power of Spirit and God, to
heal itself. Rather than merely repeating words from a book,
he began to talk about his experience. He offered guidelines
for becoming more in touch with our bodies, with our own
inner consciousness, with our true selves. He did not talk
about soul directly. He talked about how Spirit could manifest through the physical.

He said, "If you do this, that should happen." It was specific
direction. It was empirical. It was clear. I tried it. I did the

"this" he suggested and, indeed, "that" happened, just as he said it would. I was elated. I knew I had found someone who could teach me because he could guide me to new *experiences*, not just to more words and more theories. By this time in my life, I was enlivened by experience. I didn't know it at the time, but "gaining experience" is the soul's prime directive on this planet. My soul was stirring and awakening. It was longing to know itself and to know its origin, its home.

So I had found a teacher, not a spiritual teacher in a traditional sense, but a teacher who would help me to awaken to my spirit, to a deeper part of myself. I did my best to keep my mouth shut and listen to what he had to tell me. I did my best to follow his direction and to do what he said to do. I did my best for quite a while but felt I wasn't getting ahead the way I wanted. He advocated aligning oneself to the Spirit within and allowing Spirit to guide the way and to bring that which is best into one's life. I could look at his life and see that principle in action. But I could not make it manifest in my own.

One day, I asked my teacher why, when I was with him, things were smooth and my life went well, but as soon as I was away from him, I was still having a lot of personal difficulties. He said, "That which you have created prior to this time is still coming upon you." I didn't know what he meant, but then I didn't know what he meant by a lot of the things he said. So I went home and wrote those words on a piece of paper and thought about them.

A few weeks later, I asked him part two of the question: "When did I create that which is now coming upon me?" He replied, "Before you met me, before you were born on the planet this time. And before then. And before then, and before then, beyond all reasoning." I could barely believe his words. I was thoroughly and completely shaken by what he said. I could feel my blood draining down to the pit of my stomach, and I could feel my legs collapsing beneath me. It felt as if I had to consciously pull my chest in and out to breathe. I knew the truth of what he said though it was nothing I had ever considered before. I could see the implications. I knew in a flash that I had lived other times, that I had made foolish choices, that I'd involved myself in actions that had consequences I'd never considered. The magnitude of what he said—in the moment—pretty much drove all thoughts out of my mind. I don't remember much of what happened then, on the physical level. I was numb. I had no questions. I had no thoughts. I walked out and went home.

I felt hurt and betrayed, somehow, by what he told me. I thought, "How could he tell me these things?" I loved him and I trusted him, and so I thought he should say nothing that would upset or frighten me. And then I realized that I was attempting to control him just as I attempted to control so much of what went on in my life. I realized, too, that he had said nothing to hurt me; he had just stated what was true. If I took hurt from it, that was my choice. Perhaps I felt betrayed by myself. Perhaps I caught a glimpse of how I had let myself down. These thoughts occurred to me very slowly over a period of time.

Gradually, I looked at what my teacher said. I looked at my life and my actions with a new sense of responsibility. I looked at what this new perspective meant to me. Slowly, I confronted myself with my need to change, to accept the truth, to grow spiritually, to recognize my own truth, and to let go of my ego position that was so familiar to me. I realized that many people would not understand. I realized that in contrast to my previous people-pleasing behavior I was going to have to stand in my own truth, and *that* was likely not to please people much at all. This was a difficult thing to face. But I didn't seem to have a choice if I wanted to take my next step in my own progression.

After a while I went back to my teacher. I said, "Can I ask you a question?" And he said no. Tears came to my eyes. I couldn't believe I was crying. I never cried. I didn't cry for anything. But my teacher reduced me to tears by saying no. That made me extremely uncomfortable. So I went away again. I turned to other people and tried other activities. But my soul had been touched. My spiritual awakening was in process. I found that other people talked ideas, but there was no experience to match. I knew I could talk as well as anyone could. I could say all the right words. I could espouse the right ideas. I had the vocabulary down. But I wasn't having any experience. So, in defense of my indefensible position, I judged the people I was with. I also judged myself as lacking courage. I judged my teacher as rejecting me. I was locking myself into patterns of lesser and lesser quality because I was trying to equate myself with the physical world so I could feel at one with it. But it kept changing. Seasons came and went. Friends came and went. Jobs came and went. Nothing was lasting. More and more, I felt bereft. Underneath, however, I felt the stirring of a spiritual promise. I felt the sense of belonging in another way to a greater reality and to a more lasting presence.

I thought about what I had been learning about letting Spirit manifest into the physical. I thought about how I might be more in touch with my true self. I thought about spontaneity, those moments when everything comes together perfectly. I thought about moments when I was at peace with myself because I was saying what was true and behaving in a manner congruent with what I believed, and when I was at my best. Athletes sometimes talk about the "zone," which is a state of mind and body where everything seems right and success cannot be denied. Athletes say that when they are "in the zone," they know they cannot miss a basketball shot or fail to catch the ball, or they can run faster and more effortlessly than ever before. I've heard athletes describe these moments as being "moments of the soul." Students know it when something they have been struggling to learn suddenly becomes clear, and understanding floods through their whole being. Scientists experience it when, out of all they have learned and observed, a new relationship reveals itself and all the evidence falls in place to support it. Children have it when they are at their unself-conscious best. Watch a child happily playing with his mother's pots and pans, banging out his own rhythm and laughing at his own brashness, and you see that joyful spontaneity. You may well be seeing the soul. Watch a child sleeping quietly, peacefully, and you will undoubtedly be seeing the soul.

I could look at my own experiences and see the times in my life when I had been in the zone. And I could see times when I had been so far out of the zone that I might as well have been in a different universe. I tried to capture the inner experience that created the sense of connectedness, ease, and flawless timing that is indicative of being in the zone.

Loving seemed to be a key. I thought of when I used to fight with my best childhood friend. It was our loving, far deeper and more enduring than our fights, that made the fights harmless. I thought of times I'd been embarrassed as a youngster. It was the sense of oneness and loving with my friends that provided the laughter and teasing that transcended the embarrassment. When I disagreed with my parents, when I was angry with them or upset with their rules and restrictions, it was the loving that put another spin on the situation and allowed me to see their concern for me.

As I had grown older, it seemed that loving had become more and more scarce in my world. I saw much that was not loving. I experienced people struggling for supremacy, competing with one another for personal gain, and taking what they could (whether or not they had earned it). For a while, I thought that was the way it was when you grew up. I thought that loving and caring were experiences to leave behind with childhood, something the world did not value.

I didn't like that. I liked it better when there was loving in my world, in my life, in my relationships—when there was laughter and good feelings, support and kindness. I felt alien and strange in a world without loving. Gradually, I began moving toward a decision that I would not live in a world without love. What I didn't know was that love is perhaps the greatest single hallmark of the soul. The soul—that spark of the divine within each of us—reflects God's perfect love. In deciding that my world must have love in it, I was choosing my soul. I was choosing God and Spirit. I was making a choice to return "home" and claim my spiritual heritage.

In time, I learned that when I saw the positive qualities of loving, joy, peace, and compassion in myself or others, I was seeing aspects of the soul by reflection. The soul is not separate from, unusual, or strange to our physical reality. It is really not extraordinary. I believe we all experience our souls from time to time. I am sure that you have also experienced your soul, though you may not have identified it as such. When things in the world around you are harmonious, when you are happy and peaceful and when there is love in your life, it is relatively easy to catch the sense of your soul. It is natural that when the concerns and confusions of the world are at their least, your awareness of soul may be at its greatest. On the other hand, it is easy to lose track of the soul in the negativity of the world. When someone cuts you off in traffic or steals your parking space, how do you find loving and peace? When a spouse, a parent, or a child dies, how do you choose loving and compassion rather than anger and bitterness? These are true challenges. When you flunk a test or get fired from your job, when your wife or husband leaves you, when someone steals your money or beats you up, what is the relevance of the soul?

I believe the relevance of the soul is that it stands as a reference that there is more than the physical world. There is a greater reality. It stands as a reference for loving, for peace, and for the eternal choice we have to seek a higher expression and experience. It stands as a reference point that our true home lies beyond this level of glamour and illusion. What is the relevance of loving? I believe the relevance of loving is that it maintains your awareness of soul, and so of God, and so of yourself as a part of God.

It seems that in the negative experiences of our physical existence, most of us lose our sense of connection to soul or to Spirit; we lose our sense of being an intimate part of God. In the midst of feeling hurt and angry and upset, it is easy to forget. When we are struggling to get through each day, to compete in the world, to achieve some level of success, to protect and take care of ourselves and our families, it is so easy to forget that we are of God and loved by God.

These thoughts occurred to me over time and seemed to come intuitively from deep within me. I thought about my teacher and how he had refused to answer my question. I thought about my feelings of rejection, hurt, and separation. I realized that when I was not in control of the situation or getting what I wanted in the timing I wanted, it didn't necessarily mean that I was being hurt or rejected. Something else might be happening, something I wasn't entirely aware of, which might even be in my best interests. Perhaps I was being loved, not rejected. So I went back to my teacher and began to look more deeply at the idea of loving. What was loving? Was it saying what someone wanted to hear (as I'd done so much of in the past and wanted other people to do for me)? Was loving pretending that things were fine when they weren't? Was loving letting myself or someone else get away with lies? Or was loving doing what needed to be done, saying the truth that needed to be said, living from a place of integrity? The answer seemed obvious. I didn't like it necessarily, but it did seem obvious.

Loving seemed so simple, but the more I sought to be loving, the deeper it took me. I thought back to my childhood and my family. There was loving there. Things weren't perfect, but we were connected. We were a family together. I thought of the fights with my friends and my brother and how I could still feel connected to them because, beyond the fighting, we were together as friends and brothers. My father didn't always tell me what I wanted to hear. My mother didn't always allow me to do what I wanted to do. Yet I didn't doubt their loving, and I experienced the deep connection I had to them. Where had I gotten the notion that if people loved me, they would let me get away with whatever I wanted? From my mind, perhaps, or from my ego. Not from my soul.

I thought about Spirit. I thought about what my teacher was attempting to impart to me: the experience of myself as part of a greater Spirit, not merely a collection of bones and muscles and thoughts. He was teaching the integration of all aspects of being, the interrelationship among all the seemingly separate aspects of a human being. What I had put into practice of his teachings proved valid, although there were other areas I had not yet worked. In order to assist myself in aligning more with his teachings, I began to read outside sources—information on Spirit, on the presence of Spirit in man, on healing, on extraordinary powers—anything that might give me greater understanding of the human being as a spiritual being.

To my surprise, I found stories of Spirit and soul everywhere. It seemed to be a universal experience. Nearly all mythology —stories told in ancient civilizations when there may not have been a written language—speaks in some way of Spirit and soul. There are stories of miraculous healings, of transformations, and of transcendence. I read creation myths from Africa that said once God made man, He sighed and with that sigh or breath, He gave a part of Himself into man, and that is man's soul. These myths are from cultures seemingly very different from ours yet are so similar to the story of creation told in the Judeo-Christian tradition. In the East Indian culture, from which have come many great mystics and spiritual masters, it has long been believed that the existence of God is individualized within each person, and it is to the God within that each person longs to return. Men and women everywhere have a longing to go "home," to be reunited with the Source. Hence the yearning of mankind for all things spiritual. Japanese Shinto teachings speak of the *KA*, the spirit that lives within each person. The Egyptians speak of the *BA*, which is more or less the same. Chinese teachings speak of the *Tao,* an energy of harmony and oneness signifying a union with a force beyond the earthly plane. In the Bible, it says that God created man in His own image. This supports the idea of oneness and the belief that within each man and woman there is a spark of God we call the soul. I realized that the Judeo-Christian teaching, my original tradition, in essence has the same basic premises as most of the other beliefs I was reading about from other cultures, other times, and other places. There is a Creator who loves and cares about mankind and has imparted to every individual a part of its essence. This Creator is so powerful that when a human being is in touch with that part of himself that is of the Creator, he is also powerful in his creations here in this world. He can bring order to his world and his environment. He can bring order to his body, to his mind, and to his emotions. I began to realize more of what my teacher was telling me.

Certainly, since the very beginning of time, it has been obvious that there is something present in living men that is not present in those not living. And when I say "men," I speak of all mankind, which includes men, women, and children. In living man, there is animation, a life sense, a spirit that activates him and allows him activity on this earth. When that something is no longer present, that individual exists no more in this realm. And mankind seems remarkably united in the idea that there is something beyond the physical realm, that there is a Creator or a Source of some sort. Of course, what that is and how it manifests and what, indeed, lies beyond the physical world is a subject with seemingly infinite interpretations and variations. There is practically no agreement beyond the very basic notion of God and soul. But I consider the lack of agreement to be attributable to the mind of man and probably not reflective of the constancy of God. Beyond all the differences, the underlying concept is strikingly similar, and it clearly suggests that men and women—worldwide and throughout all time—have experienced something within themselves that simply is greater than the sum of their earthly experiences. Enough people over enough time have experienced something of a transcendental nature to say with certainty that "something else is going on here."

The more I read, the more it seemed that everyone but me already knew about the soul. William Wordsworth in *Intimations of Immortality from Recollections of Early Childhood* wrote:

> Our birth is but a sleep and a forgetting;
> The Soul that rises with us, our life's Star,
> Hath had elsewhere its setting,
> And cometh from afar:
> Not in entire forgetfulness,
> And not in utter nakedness,
> But trailing clouds of glory do we come
> From God, who is our home:
> Heaven lies about us in our infancy!

Oscar Wilde in his letters wrote: "To deny one's own experiences is to put a lie into the lips of one's life. It is no less than a denial of the Soul."

Ralph Waldo Emerson in his essay *The Oversoul* wrote: "See how the deep divine thought reduces centuries and millenniums, and makes itself present through all ages. Is the teaching of Christ less effective now than it was when first his mouth was opened? The emphasis of facts and persons in my thought has nothing to do with time.

"And so always the soul's scale is one, the scale of the senses and the understanding is another. Before the revelations of the soul, Time, Space, and Nature shrink away."

And of course, when William Shakespeare wrote: "This above all, to thine own self be true; and it must follow, as the night the day, thou canst not then be false to any man," he could only have been alluding to the soul, the true *self* that is the core of a man's being.

Suddenly, I saw accounts of the soul in so much of what I was reading. I encountered stories of the soul, accounts of how people experienced their souls, scholarly theories about the soul, ideas of reincarnation, and thoughts of how the soul might evolve. I was fascinated. I found that my curiosity was truly engaged and that much of the thrill of discovery I'd had as a child was returning.

One day, I heard a spiritual teacher talk about being divine. Divine! Could I believe that? The first teacher I'd been studying with had told me that all my difficulties were because of things I'd done in the past coming back to me. I had accepted that, and the new awareness had made me more careful about what I was creating in my life. In time, I had found a new teacher, one who was a spiritual teacher. He talked of the divinity that is the heritage of all men and women. It didn't make any sense to me at all. How could I be here on Earth, in a physical body, having all these difficulties, dealing with all manner of mistakes and negative things I'd set in motion eons ago, and still be divine? Even though I was reading about the soul and was beginning to accept that there was such a thing, it was still "at a distance," and I didn't see how I—in my experience of my personality, my ego, my judgments—could be divine.

So I went to the one who was my first teacher and asked, "Am I divine?" He said, "What do you think?" I was crushed. I knew what I thought. I thought I was *not* divine. I didn't see how such a thing could be possible. I went back to the spiritual teacher who claimed he (and all mankind) was divine and said, "*I'm* not divine, and if you say I am, then you're not either because you've made a mistake." He said, "Why do you think you're not divine?" I said, "Because I asked my teacher." He said, "Did he tell you that you were not divine?" I said, "No, not in so many words"—and then I wondered about that. So I went back to my first teacher and asked, "Can a human being be divine?" He said yes. Hearing his words, I felt a ray of hope, like a ray of sunshine after eons of cloudy weather. When the soul within hears acknowledgment on the physical level of its divinity, there is great rejoicing. That was what was happening to me. There was great rejoicing deep inside me where my soul was awakening.

Being very human, however, and being very mental, I began to doubt. I denied the experience I was having, which was joyful and happy, excited and even giddily elated, and I began to look at the experience from a mental point of view. It didn't make a lot of sense. I wondered why I would be so happy at the notion of divinity. I questioned what was the good of that. I wondered if my teacher knew what he was talking about. In my doubt, I decided that I must prove once and for all whether or not there could be any truth in this idea of divinity. So I sought out the spiritual teacher (the one who taught of divinity), and I said to him, "I've left my other teacher (the first one), and I've come to you." He said, "You are stupid. You doubt your teacher so you come to me, but you are not sure of me because we have no experience together which you can trust. You are out of trust with yourself because you have left the teacher you formerly trusted, so you will be unable to find sureness in yourself. If you cannot find sureness within yourself, you will never know sureness in me or any other. Go back to your teacher. Don't doubt him. Learn everything you can from him. Then come to me."

I felt very rejected. If this new teacher was divine and he knew it, I felt like I was being rejected by God. I was very humbled. I went back to my former teacher and said, "Can I come back and study with you?" He said no. Now I was stunned. I felt I had no place at all. I was very upset. Angry, hurtful words formed in my mind. He turned to me and said, "That won't work, either." Humbled again, I asked, "Why can't I come back?" He said, "Because you have met your new teacher. He was once my teacher. He will take you as a student when you begin to acknowledge both your divinity and your humanness, when you are open to learning, when you stop thinking that you can control what is going on here."

I started to see why I was having so much difficulty. It was like a curtain slowly lifting up to reveal a stage. It wasn't all the way up, but it was starting to move. I was seeing more of the truth.

I began to study with the new teacher, even though he had not formally said that he accepted me as his student. The experience was, at first, uncomfortable because our relationship was emotionally distant. He never said anything to me. He never invited me to stay after class and talk as he sometimes did with others. He never even acknowledged my presence in the class. I was there, but it felt like I was on the outside. One day, I said, "May I ask you a question?" and he said yes. I was so thrilled to be acknowledged that I promptly forgot the question. He said, "Dummy," but he said it with such great love that I knew the loving and didn't mind the "dummy." Thank goodness, my ego didn't get caught up in the supposed meaning of the word *dummy*, and my soul felt the love. I was learning. It wasn't a mental type of learning; it was subtler than that. It was learning of the heart and of the soul. There was a hint of the loving that had been present in my family, a loving that transcended what was happening in the moment and created a sense of connection and belonging. It was continuity. And a small sense of home.

I became bolder in my explorations of Spirit and soul. I thought, if the soul is the spark of God, the part of mankind that is of God, then it stands to reason that the attributes of the soul—loving, peace, joy—would be the attributes of God. But different people, groups, and religions claim somewhat different attributes of God. Some people say that God is a wrathful God and seeks vengeance on those who disobey him, whereas others say that God is a forgiving God and gives freely of His grace and loving. Some religions speak of many gods and attribute different qualities to different gods. My thoughts swirled with all the ideas, all the implications, all the possibilities. It was all wonderfully confusing.

To minimize my confusion, I decided that I would look to my own experience, such as it was, to reveal to me what might be true. I applied my curiosity to my own experience, to see what I could discover from it. I loved the challenge. Now when my teacher said something to me that shook me or that rattled or upset my old beliefs, I welcomed my experience. I claimed and embraced whatever it brought to me, and sought to learn from it.

THE LOVE GOD HAS FOR US, *the profound loving that is held in trust for us in our souls, may be revealed to us in ways that are confusing at first. Have you ever felt ignored or rejected by someone you cared about, only to discover a deeper level of loving in that apparent slight?*

Teachers, poets, artists, philosophers, and mystics through the ages have hinted at or described qualities of the soul. How have you been able to absorb these ideas and integrate them into your personal experience? Which attributes of the soul do you most relate to?

A key aspect of Soul Transcendence is choosing. Life presents us with moments of opportunity. Choosing a different response and observing the results are elements of our learning. What in you is open to learn? What in you is curious to explore territory beyond the habitual and comfortable? It can be so challenging to sacrifice our ego positions in order to be open to the moment of opportunity, especially when that moment requires us to suspend a lifetime of beliefs. Or when it asks us to let go of our need to manipulate events, attempting to maintain our emotional comfort and mental judgments. Or maybe the moment of opportunity holds up the mirror, prompting us to see deeper levels of our personal responsibility for what is happening in our lives.

Watch for opportunities to shift from the self-righteous attitude of "I know what is going on" to a more open, more humble, more innocent stance. See if you can embrace the vulnerability that can come when you don't know what is going on. Consider challenging yourself to be open for these moments of opportunity in your own life. It can be highly adventurous. What if you started your day with an attitude of "how can I use everything today for my learning, upliftment, and growth?"

If you would know more of Soul Transcendence, be open to the spiritual teachers who come your way—whether they be in the form of spouses, children, bosses, friends, or the more formal teachers of Spirit. God will use all of these and many more to teach you and assist you to grow in soul awareness. Everyone you encounter is potentially your teacher. Every situation you encounter is an opportunity to practice the peace, loving, and joy that are the qualities of your soul's essence. And one way to fulfill these potentials and opportunities is to look upon them as divine adventures unfolding in your ordinary life.

If you would know more of Soul Transcendence, practice choosing greater alignment with the qualities of the soul.

CHAPTER SIX

TRAVELING THE INNER WORLDS

SIX

One night I prayed that I would be able to experience more fully and frequently the consciousness I had glimpsed at the time of my surgeries. That night, I experienced myself leaving my body in a more conscious and direct way than I ever had before. I could see my body sleeping in bed. I could see my apartment and the street and other nearby things. Not only could I see physical things more clearly and from a different perspective, I could see my emotions and mental processes with more clarity, detachment, and loving. It seemed that in lifting above the physical level, I could know it more fully, and that made it easier not to judge what I saw. It was magnificent. Through prayer I asked that I might grow in this ability to shift my consciousness, that I might be able to leave my body often and experience this deeper loving. Spirit answered my prayer, and I started practicing in earnest.

At first, I wasn't particularly good at it. I would manage to leave my body, and then, when I'd try to come back, my body would have become stiff and rigid. I'd try to move and I couldn't. Sometimes it was a little frightening. But when I would get scared, I would ask for the presence of beings of

Light who could help, spiritual teachers and guides; then my transition back into the body would become smoother.

I wanted to know more about the other levels of consciousness, since I had glimpsed a little of what they might be. Obviously, the physical level was only a small part of what was available. I wanted to know more about the other levels. When I met beings of Light, I wanted to know where they were from. What level of awareness did they call home? What did the existence of these levels and dimensions mean to me? What was it all about?

In order to learn more and to gain more awareness, I began a daily practice of what I called spiritual exercises. Much like an athlete who develops his physical strength and ability through daily training and practice, I sought to develop my ability to travel nonphysical dimensions by daily attention and practice. I will share with you a little of what I experienced, not all of which happened right away or at any one time. I have continued this daily practice of spiritual exercises—of traveling into spiritual dimensions—for many, many years now. The experiences are never exactly the same, though they are often similar. Many of the "places" are quite familiar to me now, and there are always new places to be discovered and explored. My experience indicates to me that the dimensions of God's universe are infinitely vast. Certainly, I have never found an end, if there even is one.

I began simply by placing my attention on my breathing. As I allowed my breathing to settle and guide my consciousness at its own pace, I would begin to move out of the physical limitations of my own body. It was as if I rode my breath by moving my conscious awareness into and then beyond it. Then and now, this tends to be a drifting, gentle, and silent process for me. Gradually, I became aware of colors, textures, and sounds that were not of this physical realm. As I moved deeper into these awarenesses, I began to know a profound peace deep within me, a deeper, fuller loving, and the purest joy I could ever have imagined. Though I was only partially aware of it at the time I began these spiritual practices, these are qualities of the soul: joy, love, peace.

As I focused on my breathing and allowed my awareness to drift from this physical level, I found that I could follow my imagination and my awareness, and they would guide me to levels beyond the physical. As I moved away from the concerns of my physical consciousness, I found that my perceptions were heightened. I could see so clearly what had previously been obscure. The solutions to concerns that had been problems for me became clear in an instant. Many times what had seemed like a problem from the physical level simply didn't seem particularly significant when viewed from a higher perspective—so it made the solution very clear. Think of it this way: when you were in high school, it may have been torturous to make a decision over what clubs to join or what team to try out for or what crowd to be involved with. But when you got to college and were facing decisions over career, job, finances, perhaps marriage, the decisions you faced in high school seemed insignificant. You looked back and realized you could have made any decision and it probably would have been all right. In a way, looking at the physical world from the perspective of a higher dimension is like that. The answers seem really easy, and a lot of times you realize that any one of several options will be all right. As my awareness expanded, I often found I could look "down" and see not only my physical body relaxed and safe in my room, but I could also see life patterns—experiences, possibilities, and relationships—that were available to me. My physical life seemed so easy from this spiritual perspective. It didn't always seem easy when I was seeing only from the physical level, but from this higher perspective, it seemed quite simple.

The more I practiced my spiritual exercises, the more my life here on the physical plane began to change. It began to reflect some of the experiences I was having during my travels. I was becoming more peaceful, even in the physical world, even on the job, even with friends and family. I saw everyday occurrences in a vastly different light, so to speak. Things that would have previously seemed random to me or without much meaning took on a new significance. I began to see how so many of my daily experiences—though they did not seem like much at the time—were designed to teach me valuable lessons. They were designed as opportunities for me to learn and grow. I began to experience more of what living life in the zone could be.

And on each level, there was valuable knowledge available to me. One of the things I learned was that the freedom with which I could travel through the dimensions was not necessarily available to all of the Light beings living on the other dimensions. For example, when I was traveling in the realm of the imagination (which in metaphysical terms has often been called the astral level), I sometimes encountered Light beings whose "home" was the astral level, but they could not travel to the dimensions above the astral. They could see and touch into the physical level (which is below the astral) but could not go higher. I knew this because when, through intention and focus, I would move from the astral level to a higher level, they would seem suddenly to lose the sense of my presence and they did not come with me. They did not move from their domain. Also, when I would return to the astral level, they would be just where I had left them. When I tried to communicate to them some of the experiences I was having on higher levels, they did not understand (much as a child might not understand if you attempted to explain college-level calculus). I realized that this earth, the physical dimension, held great opportunity because I was beginning to understand that from this physical level, many other levels of consciousness were accessible. In time I realized it is also a springboard to the soul level, to our God-source, our true home.

From the astral level, I saw that, with the proper attitude here on Earth, my life really might be quite simple. It might be nothing more than learning and expanding, holding the focus of love and Light for myself and for others. It might be as simple as living and demonstrating the wisdom of the heart, and becoming increasingly devoted to God and to Spirit and to my own soul. This sounds so easy. And from a higher perspective, it is easy. Even on the physical level, it is simple, though sometimes far from easy.

I had known for a long time that I could choose to let my mind think about negative things or direct it to positive things. I knew that I could think of a situation and project a negative image or fear on it, and all of a sudden I'd be thinking horrible things were going to happen. And so my experience would become a negative one: I'd feel fearful, upset, angry, and so forth. Or I could take the same situation and discipline my mind to think about it in a positive focus so I would see the opportunities in it. Then I'd see the challenge. I'd see how much I could grow, what good could come of it, and so the experience became a positive one. Same experience, different choice.

In the same way, I found that in my spiritual travels I could choose whether I wanted to go to a place that was relatively more negative or to the highest, most positive place I could discover. It was amazing to me. I could actually make choices to determine, or at least influence, what I wanted my experience to be. People who study and research dreams have discovered what they call "lucid dreaming," the ability people have to control their dreaming. This was similar. I kept choosing for the positive because I found that I was happier when I did. I chose positive expressions, which allowed me to experience my own loving.

Sometimes when I practiced my daily spiritual exercises, I could see in my imagination (whether real or not) this planet called Earth, and it seemed to be bathed in a deep, nurturing emerald green light. Sometimes it was as if the whole planet were breathing in this emerald green light, and I could see the light bringing healing to the planet and to the physical beings here. Along with seeing the light of the physical world,

I was also aware that I heard a sound. It was a sound much like thunder, powerful and deep. Sometimes it sounded close. Other times it sounded far away. Often it sounded like a heartbeat to me, the heartbeat of the earth—or perhaps my own. At first it came as a surprise that the dimensions through which I was traveling revealed not only images but a kind of *signature sound*. It was one of the surest ways I discovered to identify where I was.

I found that these higher dimensions seemed to reflect attributes that were quite familiar to me. In a way, I already knew the territory. I just didn't know it in the detail I was beginning to discover. Continuing my spiritual exercises, holding to my intention to discover more of God's vastness, I followed the light and the sound further in my awareness. Sometimes my vision of the physical would dissolve, the sound of thunder would become more distant, and I would begin to hear a new sound. At times, I heard a whooshing sound, which reminded me of the sound of the surf, as if thousands of waves were coming in and releasing their sound to me. It was entrancing. As I heard this sound, I also began to see new shapes, aglow with a pink and rose light force. The textures of the light and sound on this new level became vividly alive inside of me. I felt as though I was riding the light and sound, all the while just observing this new level.

Here, I saw images that seemed to be dreams of creation and of the unfinished hopes of man. This new dimension seemed to be a land of lost creativity, as though there were eons filled with material of man's imagination. I saw what seemed like endless lands of floating energy forms, a sort of holding area for psychic energy forces. All this I saw in a process of imagination and, also, with a reality and a depth that was more than imagination. I began to realize that there was an actual place that was the source of man's imagination, an outer dimension that corresponded to the inner level that we call imagination, the place of our hopes and dreams. With it came an understanding of how our imaginations are shaped.

The astral level is rich in imagination, and imagination is not always positive. On the negative side, I saw how imagination could be a block because it can reflect our own fears and insecurities. It can make them bigger and "badder" than they could ever be in reality. Used negatively, imagination can keep us from achieving our dreams by making our fear of failure more real than our commitment to success. There were places I dubbed "nightmare alley" because they seemed to epitomize all my fears and give substance to all my monsters. At times, there actually appeared to be real monsters, figures like gargoyles or fantasy figures of huge lizards, misshapen dragons, and winged creatures of destruction. If I gave them power, they were frightening. But if I focused beyond them and created images of peace, light, and loving, they dissolved. What a lesson! And what an implication for my mental and emotional "monsters" in the physical world.

As I continued my travels in this level, I found that when I held a focus of safety, when I did not succumb to the nightmares, when I held and maintained positive images, the monsters proved to be an illusion, like a trick of light and mirrors. They would be there, and then they would be gone. Have you ever had a thought that something is going to go wrong in your life—you are going to flunk the test, you are going to say something really stupid during your presentation at work, you are going to go for that shot in the basketball game and shoot an air ball instead—and then you pass the test, make a great presentation, score the two (or maybe three) points? That's just like what happens when the monsters of this realm vanish in the face of positive focus and positive imagination. The threat is there, the fear is there, the panic is there—and then it isn't, and you're through it and on to the next thing.

The discipline of this astral level is to never lose the positive focus. It is a lesson that applies equally well on this physical level.

High within this realm of imagination, I discovered a place I had heard referred to by metaphysicians as Summerland. It is a place of brilliant sunshine and aliveness. Here, the warmth of an endless summer touches the heart. I thought at first I was in heaven because it was so perfect and there was such peace. Some church services close with a benediction, "May the peace of God which passeth all understanding be amongst you and remain with you always." I've often thought this reflects or matches the quality I found in Summerland. It is the sweetest, safest, most beautiful place. Summerland looks much like some of the more exquisite places on Earth, like the Swiss Alps or Hawaii or Tahiti. It reflects the physical in the ideal. Some souls, when they have found this level, believe it is heaven because it is so beautiful and perfect and is very much the image of our most ideal and perfect thoughts of heaven. It is the positive aspect of the imagination.

As beautiful as it was, I didn't stop at Summerland in my spiritual traveling and exploration of other dimensions. As part of my spiritual exercises, I did my best to stay attuned to the experience that was unfolding inside of me. When I would take the time to turn my attention to the Spirit, blacking out my room (so no outside light distracted me), using an eye mask and earplugs and listening as deeply as possible to the spirit inside of me, I would begin to hear another sound drifting through the sound of the waves (the signature sound for the realm of imagination). This new sound—of tinkling bells or chimes—led me even higher. Again, it felt as though I was riding on light and sound into a higher level. The feeling was, for me, quite different from the realm of the imagination. And the colors that I saw here were different, also. I began to see bright orange and salmon shades of light. I was aware of a greater delicacy here. This realm no longer looked like the physical world, either. The familiar images of Earth were gone. I saw a kind of fabric, almost a web, which appeared to catch and hold feelings and emotions in suspension. I began to see that the action here was one of cause and effect, rather than the action of imagination. I felt the vibration of a karmic energy moving across and throughout these levels. I saw my own life as an action of balancing ancient creations, as the laws of karma decreed.

I remembered what my first teacher had told me, that the difficulties I had in my life were the result of what I had created in lifetimes before I met him. I could see threads of energy that were mine, extending from the past and into the future. I saw some completions I would need to make in my life. I saw that the need for fulfilling the law of cause and effect leads naturally to completion, and the process of completion leads naturally to oneness, and the experience of oneness leads to peace and loving. I saw that the law of cause and effect introduces a balancing action into every life. I saw, like ocean tides, evidence of the ebb and flow of each person's journey through life on an emotional level. I saw karmic actions from millions of existences, held here for information, education, and practice. I saw them not as negatives, but like angels at the gate, protecting each soul and directing us all with the wisdom of the past—my past, our past—and with the wisdom of the ages.

My eyes were opened to the purpose of emotions, how they hold us to the lower levels as long as we do not use them for our own freedom. I saw that when emotion is negative, it reaches out to control, to possess, to have. It restricts; it binds; it inhibits. I could see how that applied to my life. I could see that when I had sought to have something in life— be it a particular relationship or job or object—that desire restricted me and left me less free than before. I could see how people put the acquisition of *things* first in their lives, thinking this will bring them peace and happiness, only to find themselves further and further away from the happiness they seek. In a positive sense, emotion is loving, caring, empathy. It allows people to feel connected, to banish loneliness, to enhance the sense of community and oneness. I saw loving as a key to freedom. I saw that as I could love each and every action, without judgment or concern, I created my path to freedom. I saw that the soul was masterful at accepting and experiencing whatever was presented. I saw that the soul exemplifies purest loving because it does not judge any choice and recognizes that there is learning with every choice.

I met incredibly beautiful beings in this realm, beings who exemplified the peace that comes with pure loving. I saw beings who, with no hint of material possessions, lived from a place of pure loving and total acceptance. I saw that one action must be balanced with another, not as punishment, but as an integral part of God's plan and the education of each individual soul. These Light beings appeared to me in forms quite similar to a physical form but with a radiance so bright I think I would have been blinded had I been looking with physical eyes. You know how a person's eyes shine when they are in love or when they are excited or are about to receive something wonderful? Picture the most beautiful person you have ever seen, the most perfect, the most lovely. Picture them about to receive the most precious gift in the world. See them aglow with love and laughter and anticipation and joy. See the light in their eyes shining through. Now think about what a being would look like if that radiance were shining through their entire body, through their heart, their fingertips, all around their head, down the length of their body. Think of that and then think of increasing it one hundredfold. You're not even close, but you're closer. And in this realm, beyond the brilliance of the images, there is a sweetness and a peace that is, again, a hundredfold, a thousandfold, of what we experience here on Earth. Think of the most sacred, special holiday time spent with the dearest of your family or friends, where you know you are loved and safe and valued, no matter what. Think of candles lit, soft music, the smell of your favorite foods being prepared, everything just the way you want it. That's getting close to the experience of this realm of emotion. When you're there, you think you could stay forever.

T HE EARTH SEEMS TO BE SOMETHING LIKE A CLASSROOM, *and each person (soul) comes to this level with very particular lessons to learn, based upon the cumulative results of their past actions. The nature of a classroom is to bring learning to areas that have been in ignorance. The nature of the law of cause and effect (karma) is to bring balance and completion to that which has been out of balance. The soul seeks completion because it wants to experience the fulfillment of its own nature— freedom, loving, joy, compassion.*

When you look at the patterns of your life within the law of cause and effect, you can often identify the learning. If you can't keep a job, rather than blaming your employers, you might ask yourself what you can learn from the situation. Maybe you need to learn tolerance, patience, or cooperation. Maybe you need to learn how to see a situation from a point of view other than your own. What you are balancing might

be attitudes of control or superiority. If you fight with your
loved ones, rather than blaming them, look for the lesson you
need to learn, what you can do differently. Look to see how
you can bring peace and harmony to the relationship. Ask
yourself what behavior you can change.

When you realize that your life does not unfold accidentally
or randomly but with meaning and purpose, you can begin
to look for the cause of the effect. As you become more
responsible for your expression and behavior, you may start
to choose your actions more carefully. Maybe you choose
peace, though you could have expressed againstness. Maybe
you choose kindness when you could have chosen sarcasm,
or tolerance when you could have chosen impatience. When
you choose those things that are positive in nature, you are
choosing your soul.

If you would practice Soul Transcendence, look for the
choices in any situation you experience. See how many
choices are available to you. The more choices you can see,
the greater is your freedom. In practicing Soul

Transcendence, look for ways to increase your altitude. How can you see your life and your choices more clearly? How can you see positive outcomes in the face of evidence that looks negative?

Choosing the most loving response available to you sets you on the path of Soul Transcendence.

CHAPTER SEVEN

THE VALUE OF INTENTION

On each spiritual dimension to which I traveled, my growing awareness was accompanied by lessons of great significance to the physical level. This continues to be so, even today, as I continue to visit all of these dimensions. In each, there is always much to be learned. These levels of consciousness are available to everyone who will take the time and expend the effort to make the visit. In their way, they are nothing special, as they are each person's natural inheritance, though of course, they are precious beyond all the diamonds and gold of this realm. A number of spiritual traditions of the East teach of dimensions beyond the physical. Numerous Eastern masters have spoken of their travels to these realms. Some masters who are able to manifest physical objects seemingly from nothing are also masters in these other dimensions. It is their mastery of the higher levels that makes it possible for them to do "miracles" here because, though the laws of the physical realm apply to *this* level, there are realms beyond the material world where our physical laws do not apply. There are many teachers of meditation who have experienced these other realms, and they present techniques for traveling to their students. Some teach how to travel only to a certain level. Some teach how to connect to your astral body or to the emotional "body." Some teach, as I now do, techniques for awakening the soul and using the soul as the vehicle to travel through these other dimensions.

Experience goes on and on infinitely (as far as I can tell at this point in my life), and there is always more to learn. Loving can always be deeper. Compassion can always be greater. Becoming aware of patterns of imagination or patterns of emotions continually brings greater understanding, empathy, and clarity. I have found no dimension to be static. It is all dynamic, in a state of change, growth, and evolvement. The Light beings, the masters and teachers of other dimensions, have revealed much wisdom to me. I have found that communication there is so clear and irrefutable. On this physical level, in our human consciousness, we have our minds to think up questions. We doubt things and we argue with what is told or shown to us. On the spiritual levels, there is much less of that quality, and what is revealed is simply there.

Look at it this way: on the physical level, when you see a chair in the room, you rarely doubt the existence of the chair. There it is. You see it. You know it. In the spiritual dimensions, what seems like an idea to us here, appears there as a chair would appear on this physical level. It is simply there. Its truth is self-evident. There is little room for questioning, doubt and some of the other patterns that are so common to the mind of man.

As my spiritual journeys continued, the salmon/orange light of the emotional level faded, and I began to see a rich, clear blue light leading me to a higher plane. The sound of the bells tinkling gradually gave way to a new tone, and I began to hear what I might call a "water song." The clear sound of running water filled my awareness. I could feel it cleansing all of my consciousness, deeply, purely. I felt as though I was drinking sound and light. I could feel the crystal clarity of this level being assimilated and absorbed by my consciousness, and I realized I was in a high dimension of mental purity and integrity. Pure intelligence surrounded me and vibrated through me. Immediately, I saw how mental processes can produce either freedom or restriction. I saw how people can create obsessions, compulsions, and mental imbalance. I saw how people can create brilliant new ideas and conceive new solutions for the benefit of themselves and others. As with the other levels, I saw that the mental process can be used in *positive or negative ways.*

On the mental level, there is a purity of thought and idea. There is a sense of infinite wisdom and a sharpening of individual thought and sense. I experienced my judgments dissolving in the energy of positive neutrality. I felt my consciousness quickening. The beings I encountered in this level did not have as defined a form as in the other levels. But I was becoming more attuned and more able to discern subtle energies and the presence of consciousness even when not necessarily accompanied by a form.

We are so accustomed, on the physical level, to not perceiving a consciousness or an intelligence unless there is a form to go with it. On other levels, consciousness *is*, whether or not there is a "form" we would recognize as a form. There may still be a form, however, one that is not readily recognizable to the physical senses. My abilities to perceive were becoming more and more refined. I had learned to see in a different kind of way that might be more akin to sensing or intuiting.

I struggle for words to describe these experiences, these realms, and these beings, because the vocabulary of this physical level does not do them justice. We simply don't have the words to adequately convey levels as delicate, as intricate, as subtly patterned as these. Throughout this book, I do my best to give you a sense, but only when you have similar experiences will you know what I am trying to say. I could give you endless detail, but it would always be somewhat inaccurate, and you could then think of endless questions. You might think of this book more like a recipe book. I tell you, as best I can, the ingredients that I used to make my cake, and then you can experiment to see if your cake can be made with the same ingredients or if you want to change the recipe a little.

All of these travels to, through, and into the higher dimensions took place over quite a bit of time. It was a gradual process. There were often new discoveries, and there was also much repetition. It reminds me of when I was a child and I explored the trails and the backcountry in the mountains near my home. At first, I explored only a little bit of a well-traveled trail. When that was familiar, I'd go a little farther. When a greater distance had become well-known to me, I'd hike off the beaten path to follow a deer, to find a spring, or to see a meadow. This new kind of traveling—traveling through spiritual realms—was much like that. I explored a little at a time, sometimes stopping to observe something in great detail, sometimes moving on.

I discovered that I could use the energy, the vitality, and the strength that were part of my physical being to propel my travels through the spiritual dimensions. It seems to be one of the advantages of having a physical body and part of what allows a greater freedom of movement through the realms. Communication with the Light beings of the other dimensions continues to be exciting, relevant, and direct. Here on Earth, the images we use to communicate are so limited by comparison and so cumbersome. If I want to show a child an image of the Earth, for example, I must find a map or a picture or perhaps take the child up in an airplane. As an idea, if I were in another dimension and I wanted to tell someone about the Earth, the image would simply be there—100-percent available to me instantly and in as much detail as necessary.

Learning in the spiritual dimensions becomes an intensely personal experience. There is nothing abstract about it. What you learn happens to you. Actually, this is the way it is here on Earth, also, though we often try to make it abstract and we then miss the point. For example, if you have a series of car accidents in a fairly short period of time, there is likely a lesson in that for you. If you persist in thinking of the car accidents as separate, unrelated incidents or as being someone else's fault or having nothing to do with you, you make your experience abstract and you miss the lesson. There are many books available now on the relationship among the mind, body, and spirit, and all of them attempt to show us how our experience is our schoolroom. This concept is still ridiculed by many in our society, but that does not make it any less true.

Knowing that lessons are available everywhere while traveling through the spiritual dimensions, if I encountered any beings or any place that seemed unloving, negative, disturbing, or potentially hurtful, I moved on. My method for moving on was to consciously remember my *intention* to be a part of only that which is loving and mutually uplifting, to ask for the presence and protection of the supreme God and those who are His representatives, to focus on the most pure Light available to me, and to use the vitality of my physical body to lift myself higher.

The experiences I have had in these spiritual realms of Light are transcendent, not of this world, and magnificent beyond my power to describe.

A S YOU READ JOHN-ROGER'S STORY, *are you sensing or experiencing an inner awakening? Can you sense a flickering interest (or more) in these ideas of soul and Soul Transcendence? Do you feel yourself wanting to reach for more? If so, you might consider that your soul is recognizing itself, its experience, and something of its journey. You may be "coming to your senses" and feeling a desire to turn your feet toward home.*

Soul Transcendence is a simple path. There is nothing extraordinary you need to do. Simply open your awareness to all that is around you and all that is within you and follow the loving.

Within yourself, open your awareness to the movement of your soul. You may find yourself wanting to be quiet so you can listen to the Spirit. You may find yourself experiencing moments of peace so profound that you experience divinity.

You may find joy appearing spontaneously from so deep inside that you marvel at its presence. You may find yourself literally seeing flashes of light bouncing across your inner or outer vision or hearing the subtle sounds and tones of the higher realms as your awareness shifts from here to there. You may choose to start a journal, to record for yourself the experiences you are having of Soul Transcendence and to encourage yourself in your journey home.

If you would tread the path of Soul Transcendence that leads toward home, make it your intention to be a part of only that which is loving. Ask to be guided and directed in your intention.

CHAPTER EIGHT

MY KINGDOM FOR A HORSE

EIGHT

Another far memory I have is of an existence long ago when I was on what might be called a spiritual path and professed to be learning the ways of Spirit, but at the same time, I was very caught up in the world, my own ego, and in my search for recognition. In that existence, I was the disciple of a magnificent master, a guru of great renown. I loved him with all my heart and I saw his magnificence, but I was not yet able to see that my own ego was preventing me from truly living the spiritual life he exemplified. In that time, I lived in an ashram (a community of devotees or disciples of the master), and I had become an important person in the ashram's administration. All the people who studied with this master teacher knew me, and they knew that I was the one closest to the teacher. It was an important position, and not only did I play on that recognition, I encouraged it. I liked it. It kept my ego satisfied. But it didn't do much for the Spirit inside of me. After the work of the ashram was done for the day, when I tried to meditate, when I tried to reach beyond the boundaries of my physical being and be in communion with a greater

Spirit, I felt fallow and empty. My meditations were dry. There was no spiritual vision.

So one day I asked my teacher, "Why is it that I do not see you?" meaning I did not see him in my meditations, in my inner vision or awareness. He replied, "You see me. You see me every day." I said, "I agree I have access to you physically. I do see you every day. I can ask you anything. You are gracious and always give me your attention. But when I am not with you physically, I do not see you. Then I feel empty." He said to me, "But that is what you have wanted. You have wanted the recognition of the physical body, and so you have given up the other."

It hurt to realize that in demanding the recognition of the physical body—mine as well as his—I had denied myself the greater experience of Spirit. I had listened to my guru's teachings for many years. I had heard him speak of God and of the great Spirit that God sends to man to be his comfort on the journey back into the supreme Source of all, the soul's true home. I had heard him speak of man's soul as being his own individual spark of God, placed deep and safe within him, to guide him home. It follows that, if the soul is of God, then all souls share a oneness, and it is that oneness that is our connection and our communion. But I had been so wrapped up in the physical aspects of my job that I had never thought about the teachings in much depth. So I had never realized that my demand for recognition in my world was blocking me from knowing the Spirit more completely. The soul does not seek recognition. The soul knows itself and God. It does not need recognition or honor here in the world. The soul is simple and pure. When I demanded recognition, I moved away from any awareness of the soul. I began to see how I had missed the point. Even though I said I wanted to know God more fully, I had not behaved as if that were true. It was "lip service" only, with no content behind it. In this false behavior, I had denied myself.

It was not too long before my teacher sent me on an errand. In that time, there were no motorized modes of transportation, no cars or trains (much less airplanes). It was in a time when travel was accomplished primarily on horseback. My teacher's errand was to travel to a faraway country and purchase horses for him and for the people of his ashram. This was a mission of great responsibility. In the past, he had gone on these types of journeys himself. It was a great honor to be trusted as one who could go and do business in his name. I felt that I had been found true, trustworthy, a worthy student and disciple. I was flattered. My ego—that part of me that fueled my work in this world—was inflated with the importance of my new position. I was very joyful because I had been chosen by my teacher.

What I didn't know was that his sending me on that journey had little to do with any of the things I thought it did. It didn't mean that I was a particularly good disciple or student or that I was particularly trustworthy. What it really meant was that he was responding to my barely articulated request to know my soul more deeply, to know our oneness more fully, and he was sending me away from him so that I might learn these things.

But I was ignorant of these motivations. And so, imbued with an inflated sense of self-importance, I set out on my journey, which would last several years. I had an appropriately large entourage, as befitted the representative of the great guru or teacher. We had supplies, rations, tents, extra animals, cooks, and so forth. We had been gone several days when I realized that I had a question to ask my teacher. I thought about the question, which seemed important, and believed that I must have an answer from him. And because I was not adept at attuning myself to our oneness or receiving spiritual answers inwardly, but only knew how to ask questions of his physical form, I felt I must return to the ashram so I could settle this question before I went any farther.

I called a halt to the journey and had camp set up. Then I took the fastest horse and, leaving at night, rode at high speed all night back across the desert to reach my teacher. When I arrived at the ashram the next day, I was exhausted. My horse was exhausted. I sat at the feet of my teacher and received his benevolent attention and the answer to my question. I left as soon as I could and, with a new horse, rode back as fast as possible to be with our people and to shepherd them on their way.

But it wasn't too many days before I thought of another question that needed to be answered (or so I thought). We were now even farther from the ashram, but I felt that I must return, not only to have my question answered but just to be with my master for a short time. I missed his physical form so much. The reality of our separation was becoming very clear to me, and I did not see how I could be separated from him for a year or even longer. So again, I had camp set up, left my people, and, with the fastest horse, set out once more, back across the desert. I rode all night and part of a day, and when I reached the ashram, I more or less collapsed at the feet of my teacher. Other students praised me for my devotion to my guru. Once more, I received his kind attention, and he answered my questions. The next day, I rode at top speed back to camp, and then we all resumed the journey.

One more time, a week or so later, I rode back to the ashram to be with my teacher. By that time, the distance was so great that I arrived in a serious state of exhaustion. I said to my teacher, "I can't go back." He called other students in and said to them, "Put him on a litter and take him back. He has a job to do and he cannot forsake it." I pleaded with him, saying, "But I am ill." He said, "By the time you are back with your group, you will be well enough to resume your responsibility." I knew that if I went back, I would have to complete the journey without seeing my teacher again until it was done. I was desolate. I did not see how I could survive such a separation. They put me on a litter, and we began the trek back to where I had last made camp. I kept thinking I would sneak off in the middle of the night and ride back to the ashram. But I knew I could not. I knew I would not be welcomed again until the journey was complete.

The people who were responsible for delivering me back to the group said to me, "Why did you do this? Why did you break your body down so that we have to take care of you now?" I said, "I did it in devotion to my teacher." That was not true, yet the truth was beginning to dawn on me. I began to see that I was simply afraid of the emptiness I felt inside when I was not physically in his presence. I began to realize that I would have to be devoted to my teacher by being devoted to myself, by handling my levels of responsibility. I began to think about the things he had been teaching me about Spirit, about soul, about oneness. I began to realize that if he were truly omnipresent as he said he was, he could be here in the desert with me as well as at the ashram. I certainly didn't have that experience yet, but I was open to the possibility. True, my awakening was born of desperation. But the motivation for awakening hardly matters. The fact was that I was awakening to something I had not known before.

I realized that sending me on the journey was an act of devotion—his toward me. He was devoted to teaching me about Spirit as he had said he would. When I realized the journey was my lesson, I embraced it as best I could. When I reached my destination, I was humbled enough to simply complete the negotiations and, without fanfare, purchased the horses that were required. I did it anonymously. I said only that I was representing one who needed good horses. I got good deals, good prices on the horses. If the sellers had known they were for my teacher, they might have asked higher prices because he was well-known. As I began the journey back, I realized I had omitted the name of my master not as any sort of guise or tool of negotiation, but because it had simply not occurred to me to use his name. In retrospect,

I wondered if I had failed because I had not transacted the business in his name.

It was just about that time that my teacher appeared to me inwardly in his radiant spiritual form. I was awestruck. I had never experienced anything like this. I could sense his presence. It was magnificent. I could see his Light. I could feel his loving. I felt his spirit not only within me but all around me. It appeared to be in the trees, in the rocks, and in the very air. I saw his spirit in all the people around me, in the animals, and in the earth. It was everywhere. I knew that I was a part of him, as he was a part of me. I knew that he was a part of what we might call God—and that since he and I were one, I too, must be a part of God. It was an experience of my soul. It was an experience that lifted my awareness well beyond the world and the concerns of the ego here. I realized that in the past, when I had plied him with questions, they had been questions of the ego. They had been my ego saying, "Recognize me. Let me know you know I am here." And all along, we were present together in the greater reality of soul. Where I had thought there was separation, there was none.

I was transformed through that one experience. There were many more. My inner awareness of my teacher's presence and spirit grew daily. I was awakening to my soul and to God as the source of my soul. I became more joyful, more peaceful, and more loving. Each day became an inner adventure.

The journey back to the ashram took about two years more. In that time, I discovered that the grace of the master was sufficient to sustain me in my awareness of my soul, of God, and of his spiritual form. I needed nothing else. I was content. I entered into a state of peace. I knew that God was present within me, as well as within all other beings and forms on Earth, and I knew the oneness. It was blissful. I could sleep by myself in the middle of a desert. I could sleep on a horse. I could sleep with hundreds of other people. It didn't matter. I was with myself. I was with my spiritual master, and I was with God.

Some of the people who were with me on the journey took advantage of my new state of peace, and as I was no longer seeking to control them or make myself greater than they, they took the opportunity to belittle me. It wasn't fun, but I realized they were creating separation with their egos. Previously, it was my ego that sought recognition and needed to feel greater than others, which created separation. Now, they sought to make themselves greater than me, which also created separation. I knew this. I knew the separation was false and unnecessary, but since I had so recently been playing the other role, I just let it be. A part of me briefly wondered about getting even when I got back to the ashram. But I realized that when I got back to the physical presence of my master, I would do nothing but what I was sent to do, which was to serve the highest good. And that certainly did not include getting even.

The journey home wasn't all easy. There were many difficult moments, moments when people were upset, moments when the animals were sick, moments when I thought everything would fall into disaster. Sometimes I doubted myself. I doubted my ability to shepherd the group home and my ability to complete the journey. Through it all, I simply did my best to keep moving forward, making some progress each day, dealing with the challenges that arose as best I could.

When, after many months, we finally came within sight of the ashram, there was great rejoicing in the group. There was great joy that the journey was done and we were home. There were those who could not wait to present the horses we had purchased to the teacher, and they took the horses and rode immediately into his presence. I went instead to my small quarters to get cleaned up and to prepare the record of the journey for my teacher.

In a short while, as I was working, my teacher came to me. I was surprised. I said to him, "I was preparing the record to bring to you. Why did you come to me?" He said, "Never before have you given me a chance to come to you. You always came to me first. Often I have wanted to come here, to be with you, to talk with you and share food with you. But you have not allowed it before because you have always come to me." I realized he was telling me that I was always leaving "home"—my center, my soul—to go someplace else, to go outside of myself for fulfillment, to try to be something I was not. Then he said, "Even your wife and children have been more devoted than you because they have been steadfast in taking care of all the things that were really your responsibility." With that statement, the last vestige of my ego died because, in that culture and time, to be less than your wife or less than your children in the eyes of your master was devastating.

At the moment my ego died, a very interesting thing happened. My extension to the world through my emotions also died. And then the emotions turned and moved back inside of me, back into the Spirit, and I experienced absolute bliss. I didn't know what was happening to me. All I knew was that I felt absolutely free and absolutely at one with everything and everyone. That my master was at hand was sufficient for total bliss. That my wife and children had been steadfast and did, in my place, things I should have done became a blessing, not a rebuke. That I had completed the journey and brought the horses to my master was a warm glow deep inside of me. But with it was the awareness that had I not been able to complete that journey, in terms of outer success, I would have been equally loved, equally valuable, equally honored, as was the prodigal son, though he returned home penniless and depleted.

I realized that the outer accomplishment was nothing; it was the inner accomplishment that mattered. My journey had been one of inner growth, awareness, and expansion. The purchase of the horses was just the purchase of horses. Anyone could have done that. At that moment, I realized there was nothing outside of Spirit. I knew there was divine perfection in the world and in all the experiences of this world, however they seem to be. It was a time of bliss, of joy, of loving.

In the time that followed, I watched the master serve others. I had never been aware of that before. I watched him clean up after his students, and I realized how much he had been cleaning up after me for all those years. I saw how he was of service to me when he sent me out on the journey for the horses. I saw how he served that which was highest and best in me, which was my soul. I realized his love—not just for me, but for all his students and, indeed, for all the world. His love was not limited nor was it conditional.

While I had been on my journey, my teacher had used me and my behavior as an example to teach others. When he was teaching the inner quality of the soul, he would say to his disciples, "Do you remember the student I sent to purchase the horses? Do you remember what he did, saying that it was devotion? Don't do that. Don't fool yourself by thinking you are devoted to me if you are attached to my physical form. Be devoted to the inner form that is both me and you. Be devoted to your own spirit within, to your own soul." When he said these things to the others, his love for me was so great that he would take me into the spirit of his beingness. While miles away, inwardly I would hear him say these things. And, in the hearing, I would feel the error in what I had done. I knew the error of my behavior, not only toward him but also toward the other students. I'd pretended to know more than I knew. I'd pretended to have more awareness than I did. I'd pretended a lot of things.

I knew it was important to make amends for these errors. So after I had returned to the ashram, I went to each person and spoke of my errors and offered my apologies. It was nothing anyone told me to do. It was nothing that was required from any outer authority. It was something that was important to do, from my own inner authority and for my soul. And so I completed that part of the journey, too, and came into a time of peace and honor within myself and with those around me who were also seekers on this path of awareness. My soul was awakening and I felt at home. I had left the ashram and the physical presence of my master and lived the illusion of separation, and then I had awakened to the spiritual unity and returned to the loving father (my master) and felt a spiritual communion greater than anything I had ever known.

I learned that awareness of the soul is not something that can be achieved by guile. Nor is it something that can be achieved by cleverness. To get to soul, one must go past the tools of this world—cleverness of the mind, power of the emotions, images of the imagination, strength of the body—and be honest with whatever is left. Sometimes, that doesn't look like much. Sometimes it isn't much, in terms of the world. In spiritual terms, it can be magnificent.

My far memory is a blessing to me because as I remember experiences from other times and places, I can bring the learning from *then* forward into this life *now* and save myself having to learn the same lessons all over again. In remembering, I am in touch with my soul and its journey home.

EGO IS OF THIS PHYSICAL, MATERIAL WORLD. *Ego is what gets us up in the morning and helps us accomplish in this world. In that respect, it is a blessing. Ego is also an individual process. Although it is a useful tool in its positive aspect, in its negative aspect, ego creates separation. The soul is of Spirit and the divine. The soul knows its God source and knows that it is created out of divine substance, as are all other souls. And so it experiences oneness.*

When you feel separation or loneliness, look to what your ego is doing. Is it prompting you to act as if you are greater than others? Is it judging you as being less than others? Or more than others? Or both? Are you demanding that those around you fulfill your expectations? Have you become adversarial?

Recognition has its place in this world and is fine when you can keep it in a balanced perspective. Have you sought recognition at the expense of a greater participation in soul awareness? Maybe you haven't been asked to purchase horses. But is there some assignment in your life where the stakes seem high? Could you use this as an experiment to learn about your motivation? What happens when you are willing to question your motives? What happens when you reach into "the highest good of all"?

If you would know Soul Transcendence, move your attention out of the ego and into greater honesty with yourself. More than speaking truthful words, be willing to honestly examine your motives and change your behavior in keeping with your learning. And as you move past the initial challenge this presents, you may find qualities of the soul: freedom, joy, peace, loving and . . . oneness.

If you would know more of Soul Transcendence, be willing to ask yourself, "Is this choice taking me closer to the experience of my soul? Is this choice leading me home?"

CHAPTER NINE

BEYOND THE MIND OF MAN

NINE

In the small Utah town where I grew up, the Mormon Church was just about the only church in town. That was where all my friends worshiped. That was where all the girls were. So that was where I was. I was about sixteen years old, just getting ready to graduate from high school, and part of the church youth group. My friends and I were a pretty cocky group. Those were good times—the beginning of the fifties. In those days, at least in our town, we didn't drink and we didn't smoke and we didn't chew tobacco. And there were a lot of other things we weren't supposed to do until we got married. But we still managed to have fun.

One night, in our church youth group (there were about twenty of us there that night), the leader sat us all down and passed out paper and pencils. I immediately thought this was going to be some sort of IQ test, which didn't bother me because I figured I was smart enough to do well on any test they could give me. After we had each received a pencil and a piece of paper, the leader said, "If you could have one thing, if God could give you one thing—just one thing—right now, what would it be? I want you to write that one thing on your paper." Spontaneously, I wrote, "I would like my mind to leave me alone."

After I'd written that, I thought it was sort of dumb and decided I wouldn't hand my paper in so that no one could know what I'd written. The leader said, "Okay, pass your pencils to the aisle." That was easy. Then he said, "Now pass your papers to the aisle." I was in the middle, so I thought it would be easy to fake. As the papers came past me, I'd just stuff mine in my pocket and pass the others along. But just as the papers got to me, the leader said, "Be sure you pass yours, also."

He startled me. I wondered how he could have seen me or known what I was thinking, but in a sort of reactive response, I put my paper in with the others and passed them on. After I had let go of them, I realized he couldn't possibly have seen me or meant me, but it was too late. My paper was being handed up to the front, along with all the others.

He began reading through them. Some he read aloud. One paper he set aside, and as he did, he said, "I think I found one that is absolutely profound." All the kids, including me, wondered whose paper he had set aside. We knew the ones he'd already read, so the kids who had written those weren't anticipating anything. But the rest of us knew our papers were in there someplace. So after he'd read a few more, he took the paper he'd set aside and said, "The reason I wanted to save this one for last is that I would not have thought to write this, but now that I have seen it, it would be what I would write about myself."

So he picked it up and read it, and it was mine. I sort of slid down in my chair, engulfed in feelings of embarrassment, as kids are when they are singled out in a peer situation. Then I had a brilliant thought that maybe someone else had written the same thing and it wasn't my paper after all. So I raised my hand and said, "Were there two papers that said that?" He replied, "No, only yours." I didn't know how he could have known it was mine, but thinking back, I realize that it was precisely because my mind wouldn't leave me alone that I'd even thought of that question. I had simply demonstrated what I had written. But I still wasn't 100-percent convinced until he sent the paper back to me and I'd checked to be sure it was my handwriting. That, also, was indicative of the way my mind worked. I checked everything. I still do.

The youth group leader went on and talked a little about how the mind can be our worst enemy because it can take the negativity of the world and magnify it, and repeat it, and obsess about it, until we feel like we are going a little mad. And as he talked, all the other kids kept turning to look at me. At first, that was okay, and then it wasn't, and then I just wondered if we could please close the meeting and go home. Before too long, he said, "I'd like you all to go home and think about what you wrote."

I just wanted to get out of there and go home. I was embarrassed, and I wanted to create separation as a way of protecting myself (not yet remembering the lessons from my previous life that dealt with ego and separation). As my friends and I walked outside, the other kids started asking me, "How does your mind not leave you alone?" I said, "It talks to me continuously." They said, "Does it ever tell you anything you don't know?" I said, "Never! It never tells me anything I don't know. I make up the conversations, but I make up both sides of the conversation. And then I keep thinking up more points of view and more arguments for each side, and it just goes on and on and on." Then the other kids started sharing how their minds wouldn't leave them alone either. And I was amazed to find out that something I thought was my own individual, unique problem appeared to be universal. It turned out to be a human condition. So the experience of separation yielded to the experience of connection. I learned that through connection, with communication and by sharing honestly, a oneness or a commonality revealed itself. I probably felt more connected to that group of kids than I ever had before.

That night was a turning point in my awareness because I realized there was something other than my mind that was part of my being. I realized that if I could say, "I would like my mind to leave me alone," there was something else identifying itself as "I" and "me." I wondered what or who that might be.

I began to realize that I also spoke of "my body" and "my emotions" and "my imagination." I wondered who it was that claimed possession of those elements of myself. I wondered who lay behind the emotions, the mind, the body, and the imagination. Who, I wondered, is "me"? As I pondered this question, I could feel something inside of me stirring. It was like some part of me was waking up, becoming more aware of itself. I began to have a thought: "Something else is going on here." It felt like something way beyond what could be seen in the physical world. This was the beginning of my soul awakening in this present lifetime. This was my moment of waking up and realizing that there was more to life than I had previously realized. This was the moment I heard God's question, "When are you coming home?" and realized that the physical world was not my true home. There was something more.

As children and as youngsters, we experiment with many expressions and experiences. It is one way we begin to gain identity in this world, and it is a necessary step in our evolvement. Too often, however, we do not see beyond those various expressions to our soul essence, the core or center pole of our beingness. If we become a musician, for example, we may think that without our musical expression, we are nothing; we have no value, no place in the world. If we become a teacher, we may identify so greatly with that role that we cannot see ourselves as separate from it. These beliefs are traps of this level. For our souls have expressed in myriad ways throughout the scope of time and space and remain true to their divine essence, no matter what our expression.

Soul is the essence of who we are. I believe the mind, the emotions, the body, and the imagination are "coats" we acquire when we are born to this earth. They allow us to function here in this dimension. They allow us to be seen, to move about, to relate to one another, and to have substance here. So often in life we misidentify the man or woman for the coat he or she is wearing. We don't realize that the coat may be taken off and the essence remains. We think we must have the coat to be real. There is so much in our culture and our society to support this. In other cultures, the illusions may not be as strong—or they may simply be different. As an American youngster, however, I did not yet have experiences of Spirit and soul, universal truths or teachings; I was still very much a seeker. I was looking for who I might be.

As my soul began to stir and come awake and consciously seek a path home to God, I began to feel more and more removed from this world and more "homesick" for the world of Spirit. I don't think this is unique. I think many people experience this in their lives. It often feels like something is missing. Sometimes there is a sense that we don't truly belong here. And sometimes there are feelings of sadness or despair or a sense of having an invalid life or an invalid expression. I think these feelings occur when we have separated from our soul, when we have lost track of its existence and are trying to deal with the world on its terms, rather than nurturing our connection with Spirit. The soul wants to experience more of itself because there is joy, loving, and peace. It wants to know itself and its own divinity.

As my soul responded to the question my consciousness posed—"Who am I?"—I began to search for teachers who could guide me on my journey home. I found many teachers, and in time, I found those who were to be my spiritual teachers and help me discern the "coats" that I wore and the misidentifications I had with my body, mind, ego, and desires that separated me from my soul and Spirit.

My teachers showed me that each soul has an experience uniquely its own. No two journeys are alike. The experience that my soul needs for its growth and expansion and discovery on the path home to God is not exactly what your soul will need. Each path is individual. No one but you has authority over your soul. You are the ultimate authority on yourself. Others can assist you. Others can point the way. But there is no one who will walk your path but you. Your soul knows what you need to learn in this life. Your soul knows what experiences you need to move closer to Spirit and God. If you choose those things, that is fine. If you choose other experiences, the soul will learn from those, also, though the journey home may be a longer one. There is nothing wasted. There is nothing superfluous. The soul will ultimately use every experience for your upliftment. In time, all will be used for good.

The soul is on a path of evolvement. It is seeking to return to its source, to the realm of Spirit and God. It will use all experiences to further its progress along the path. There is no experience that is useless or does not have value because, in the end, all is for the soul's experience. The ultimate purpose of the soul's original separation from the God source is to know God completely—in all its dimensions, experiences, and expressions—and it learns more through this separation than it could if it never "left home." Just as the prodigal son could never have fully appreciated his father's home if he had remained there, the soul leaves its home to travel far and wide and to know both the negative and the positive of all existence, because it is in the dynamic between the negative and the positive that there is life and consciousness.

Much of the experience of the physical earth is on the negative side. There are plenty of examples everywhere of greed, jealousy, hurt, and pain. There are examples of people wanting to gain advantage over another, wanting to gain power and control and not being too concerned about how they go about getting it. Of course, there are also examples of goodness, kindness, benevolence, and loving. I have also seen evidence of the positive and negative polarities on the higher levels of spirit—imaginative, emotional, and mental. And positive and negative polarities exist within each individual, as well. We are sometimes negative in our thinking or our emotions, and we are sometimes loving and kind in our behaviors and charitable in our thinking. It is all part of our human experience.

CONSIDER THAT FIRST AND FOREMOST
YOU ARE A SOUL, *and your personality, emotions, mind, talents, and abilities are nothing more than the various coats you have acquired on your travels here in the physical realm. Even as you wear these coats, you can experience the "you" that lies beneath them. Is there a coat you don't like? Perhaps you can forgive any experience you've judged as negative. Perhaps you can embrace it and gain the learning from it.*

Have you ever done something or said something that seemed embarrassing, only to find out that the honest expression in the moment brought a sense of closeness into the group around you? When we have the openness to share ourselves, we may learn that our expression can bridge the apparent separation to bring greater oneness. Consider that beyond your personality expression, your essence is of a higher nature, divine in its source, divine in its heritage. Consider that you are a part of God, a soul in community with all other souls on Earth.

If you have a choice in your expression, choose the positive. If you face a choice and you don't know which way to go, choose the most loving action you can perceive. Choose an action that doesn't hurt yourself or another. Choose an action that allows you to take care of yourself and help those around you in the most loving way possible. Loving and caring will lead you unerringly to the path of Soul Transcendence.

If you would know more of Soul Transcendence, reach out, connect with other people as a way to bridge the sense of separation and to experience loving and oneness.

CHAPTER TEN

COFFEE, PINEAPPLE PIE,
MY TEACHER, AND I

TEN

I continued to do battle with my sense of separation and my ego identification into the world. Even as my soul was awakening, I continued wanting to be competitive, seeking to be important, aspiring to excel, and so forth. My ego wanted accomplishment and acknowledgment. My lesson was to express more the qualities of the soul: loving, compassion, oneness, and communion.

One evening, I was with one of my spiritual teachers in a gathering with other students. After the session, I broke through and transcended my barriers of separation and said to my teacher, "Would you like to go out and have a cup of coffee with me?" He replied, "I thought you'd never ask." I was amazed. I thought about all the times I had felt rejected, hurt and pushed away, and I realized that he was just waiting to be asked. I was so elated with the thought that he wasn't rejecting me, maybe he even liked me and we could be closer, that I took off out the door, got in my car, drove down the road to the coffee shop, went in and ordered a cup of coffee and a piece of pineapple pie—and then realized that I'd forgotten to bring my teacher. I was horrified! I ran out of the restaurant, got back in my car, drove like gangbusters back to where my teacher was, ran in the door, and there he was sitting on the chair with his hat on. I just started laughing. He started laughing. We both laughed and laughed, and then I started crying as all the feelings of rejection, hurt, not belonging, feeling separated, lonely, lost, all came up and were released and healed. I think I cried about fourteen lifetimes. Then he said, "Did you pay for your pineapple pie?" That startled me all over again. I jumped up and headed out the door, but remembered to stop and ask, "Do you want to come?" He was right behind me, still laughing. We got in the car and drove back to the restaurant. The pie and the coffee were still at the table, with a second cup of coffee and a second piece of pie beside them—and the check. We sat down to enjoy the pie and coffee and the camaraderie of the moment.

Neither one of us actually ate much, but that wasn't really what the moment was about. It was about healing. It was about coming into oneness. Just being with my teacher was resolving many things for me very rapidly. I was experiencing acceptance and loving. At one point, though, as we started to run out of things to talk about, I turned to him and said, "Are you done?" He said no. So I tried to make conversation but felt awkward. After a few minutes, I asked him again if he was through, and again, he said no. I started to get tense. I couldn't identify what was happening. I couldn't find any reference points for this. It was making me nervous. Finally, I asked him again if he was finished. He said, "Does it bother you that much to have me with you in public?"

I realized I was back to my old tricks of feeling separate and so was trying to control situations and trying to make things be what I thought they ought to be, instead of just relaxing and enjoying the moment. I said to him, "It's not that. I was afraid I was inconveniencing you." He said, "Don't you think I would tell you if you were?" I said, "I'm not sure," and I could feel myself going to the back of the class really fast. Then I realized that if I looked beyond my feelings of separation to the truth of my experience in the moment, I was the one who was ready to leave. Instead of staying stuck in my feelings of separation, I took responsibility for my truth and said, "I guess you'll do what you will do and I'll do what I will do, and maybe now is the time for us to go do something else." He said, "I'm ready." And I realized I'd been asking him the wrong question. I'd been asking, "Are you through?" rather than, "Are you ready to go do something else?" Another subtle teaching: he responded simply to my exact question and so helped me be responsible for what I was asking. In not making any assumptions or guesses about what

I might mean, he waited until I made it clear what I meant. He was teaching me deeper levels of truth and integrity.

By now it was about 2:00 in the morning. We got in the car, and I asked him where he would like to go. Without a specific reply, he began directing me to drive up the block, turn left, down the next block, turn right, turn left—seemingly random directions. I started to anticipate the unexpected. I started to check all possibilities, to see if there were any cars anywhere around, so if he said, "Left" when I was in the right lane, I'd know in advance whether or not I could make the turn as directed. He acknowledged what I was doing and said, "Now you are on your way," and I knew he didn't mean physically. This was another teaching that applied on many levels. There can be no assumptions on any level about what may happen next. It's wise to be prepared. It's wise not to get stuck in a rut and forget to be aware of the changes around you. Simple "presence" is another quality of the soul.

Before I took my teacher home that night, he said, "When we first drove away from the coffee shop, I said to turn right and you didn't because you had not looked for yourself to see that the way was clear. Did you think that I would run you into something that would hurt you?" I said, "I guess so because that's why I didn't turn." That was an honest answer. The truth. He asked, "Do you really think I would do that?" I said, "When I think about it, no. But by my actions, yes, that is what I thought because I did not make the turn as you directed." Another honest answer. In the time we talked, I found I had driven him to his home, without being consciously aware of where he lived. As my ego had dropped away and I was able to be honest and true with my teacher, I had let fall the barriers that kept us separated in consciousness. With our consciousness as one, communication was effortless. I let him out at his door and said, "I'll see you later." He said, "You have learned what I can teach you." And I replied, "Okay." There was no rejection, no question, no hurt. Truth. My teacher had opened my awareness of other levels and had given to me the gift of connection, not only on this physical plane but on other planes of awareness as well.

I was learning to let go of the ego, to seek inner riches rather than the riches of the world. I was seeking inner strength rather than ego strength in the world. I knew that the inner strength and wisdom would, through a natural process of evolvement and awakening, move out into the world in its own timing. Intuitively, I knew that as I gave my strength back into myself, to my soul, I came closer to God and to the peacefulness that is of God. I knew this was the path home to God.

THE SOUL DOESN'T HAVE TO "LOOK GOOD," *impress others, protect itself, or lie to get ahead. It reflects a purity that is of God. It reflects the simplicity of Spirit. This simplicity is often found in the quality of being present. When we are present in the moment, we find that life works so much better. Our hidden agendas of controlling others' responses create separation, which creates tension, which, in turn, creates more anxiety about our performance. The soul isn't interested in this kind of performance. It is attuned to the truth that is found in simplicity, in authenticity. When innocence is present, it is easy to be authentic. When innocence is present, we are not trying to impress. We are living genuinely and with integrity. With these values, we can be relaxed. Then, as we cooperate with what is present, we find ourselves in a flow. We discover that life is unfolding in small miracles of perfect timing. It is the timing of the soul.*

Let's say you are here in this world to learn how to drive. These lessons may encompass many aspects of the territory you drive in: the way the streets are laid out, traffic laws, local customs, and much more. Imagine that your soul, sitting in the passenger seat, knows the best way home. Consider being patient and trusting of your soul's direction. Ask in simplicity, "Where shall we go?" See how skilled you can become at listening and then following the "left," "right," "right again," and "steady as she goes" directions your soul is giving you.

Cultivate openness in your approach to life, in your expression, and in your relationships. Explore the simple honesty of the moment. Ask, "What is present for me right now? And what is my soul's direction for me right now? What is the most authentic and loving way of expressing this?"

If you would practice Soul Transcendence, seek to be honest and genuine in your daily life.

CHAPTER ELEVEN

NAVIGATING THE INNER REALMS

ELEVEN

As time went on, the process that I would come to call Soul Transcendence began to emerge more and more clearly. Through study with my spiritual teachers and through my own process of spiritual exercises, I learned how the soul is present and expressing both here on the physical level and in other dimensions of consciousness. I learned of places that exist objectively outside of the physical earth that correspond to our levels of inner consciousness. I've told you about some of my travels in the astral level and in the realms of emotion and mind. There were more realms to be discovered.

I learned that the experience of the soul is part of everyone's experience, whether or not we are aware of it. Everyone on the planet is manifesting through soul. Or should I say that every soul on the planet is manifesting in a physical body? The more we identify with the soul, the more we identify with the eternal and the qualities that are everlasting. If we identify with the physical body (which is not eternal or everlasting), there is always going to be someone who comes along with a stronger body or a more beautiful one. Or time simply catches up with us, and we wake up one day and wonder what has become of us. If we identify with the mind and pride ourselves on our intellectual capacity, there will always be someone who will come along and be more brilliant. This world is not designed for permanence. It's all temporary. To know more of the soul, it is important to look beyond the illusions of the mind, the body, and the emotions.

Even peace and tranquility are temporary states in the physical world. We get them periodically to regain balance. But there is always something that comes along to change that condition. One skill you can develop is the ability to get back to a place of peace and tranquility more and more quickly. You can become so good at this that the times you experience disturbance or confusion begin to look infinitesimally small. Loving, however, does not have to be temporary. It is a quality that can sustain itself through all situations, as can all the qualities of the soul. When you are loving, you are most closely in contact with your soul.

In the time I studied with my spiritual teacher, I became aware that I had many dreams with him. At first, I thought these were just ordinary dreams, and I didn't give them much credence. Then one night, I dreamed of meeting a magnificent being from another dimension. In my dream, the being appeared in the form of a man, but a radiant, magnificent man. He was dark skinned, his face narrow and intense. His eyes were dark brown, nearly black, and luminous. In the dream, he was clothed in robes of brilliant blue. The next time I saw my teacher, and before I said a word, he asked me how I had enjoyed meeting the master form. And he described the man in my dream with total and quite startling accuracy. I was dumbfounded and thought about the implications of him knowing about my dream and the possibility that it was not a dream at all.

Another time, in the early morning hours, I felt myself moving out of my room, lifting up in space. At first I could not tell if I was moving physically or only in my perceptions. It felt very real. I experienced movement for a short time and then stillness. I didn't know what to do, so I did my best to keep my awareness present in the stillness. And then I quite literally heard my teacher say to me, "What do you see?" I replied in my thoughts that I did not see anything. He said (and I could hear the smile in his voice), "Open your eyes." Oh! I opened my eyes and still did not see anything but a kind of luminous white fog all around me. When I woke up in bed a few minutes later, I thought the entire episode was nothing more than a dream, until I looked outside and saw that there was very dense fog that morning. I realized that what I had seen in my "dream" was just exactly what I was seeing in physical reality. I was even more surprised when I saw my teacher later that day and, with a smile and a twinkle in his eyes, he asked if I'd enjoyed my journey through the fog that morning.

I was amazed. Were these dreams or memories of other, nonphysical experiences? I discovered that my teacher was able to tell me of numerous dreams I'd had, and he sounded as though he was simply recounting experiences we had shared. Perhaps it was so. If we shared experience in dreams, however, I wondered what the mechanism was, as our physical bodies were obviously sleeping in separate locations. Was it our souls that shared the experience of dreams? Was the physical body simply a tool for experiencing the physical level? Did we possess other "tools" for experiencing other levels?

As I went forward in my spiritual studies, I had so many questions. I found my thirst to know could not be quenched by words or theories. It was quenched only by experiences that showed me the true answers. Sometimes those experiences happened here on the physical level. Sometimes they happened on other levels. I began to remember more and more and more of what happened on the other levels, in my dreams, in other nonphysical modes of awareness.

Then, after my surgeries and my awakening to realities and dimensions of awareness beyond the physical, I began to explore and look beyond my physical senses in a more active and directed way. I began to experiment with what existed beyond what I could see, hear, taste, think about, feel, imagine, and so forth. I began to pay some attention to what it was that seemed to do all of these other things or who it was that seemed to have these other experiences. Every time I attempted to see beyond myself, I came back to my breath. It seemed like my breath was the simplest element of myself.

I began to know that my breath was intimately connected to my life, life force, and spirit. I understood that everything that breathes has life in it. I became aware that when my mind quieted down, there was my breath. When my physical body was in pain, sometimes it was all I could do to maintain my breath. In those moments, breathing became all-important. I knew that as long as I had breath, I had life. I had learned this very powerfully during my surgeries. I thought about the passage in Genesis in the Bible that reads, "And the Lord God formed man of the dust of the ground, and breathed into his nostrils the breath of life; and man became a living soul." I realized that life is, indeed, a gift from God through the breath. The soul is activated by the breath. I thought of people who are paralyzed in some part of their bodies, due to situations of their birth or physical types of accidents. Though they might not have mobility in the way many people do, it doesn't make them any less alive. It doesn't make them any less able to participate fully in this experience called life. There is life when there is breath. Where there is breath, the soul is present and involved in the experience of learning and growing in the myriad of ways available to each person. It is not any *particular* experience that creates life. What makes a life is that each one of us has received the most precious gift from God, the gift of soul. When we have that, we have life. What form that life takes is a process of many decisions and choices.

Sometimes, as I experimented with spiritual exercises, I would be very quiet and simply focus on my breathing, and I would allow myself to gently wonder about the universe and mankind's place in it, and my place in it. I would think about what I had learned from my teachers and the implications of the spiritual teachings. I would begin to feel a sense of expanded awareness. I would do my best to establish a connection with the sense of spiritual promise I sometimes felt. Often I would listen inwardly for the signature sounds of the higher realms or look for the familiar images of those realms. I would focus my awareness as deeply and silently within my consciousness as I could and then let it go.

It became clearer I was hearing sounds that did not have their origin in the physical plane. I was aware of light and of changes in the light on my inner vision (what I was "seeing" with my eyes closed). I wondered what I could possibly be experiencing. Being skeptical by nature, at first I thought I was seeing lights from the street, from cars, or lights from other buildings. I might be hearing sounds from the physical environment. So I ran all sorts of tests and experiments to be sure I wasn't fooling myself. I would black out my room so there could not possibly be any light from an outside, physical source. I would check to see whether or not the neighbors were home so I would know if something I was hearing might be coming from next door. Sometimes I used cotton in my ears or earplugs. Sometimes I used eye masks. I tried all sorts of things. And when I had controlled my environment as completely as possible and was sure that the sensory input from this physical level was nil, I found that I still had the experience of seeing patterns of light, hearing patterns of sound, and sensing changes that could not be accounted for on the physical level.

Needless to say, I found this interesting. I was most certainly intrigued. By focusing my awareness and concentrating simply on the experience within my consciousness, I began to follow what I heard and what I saw, to see if it had a source and, if so, what that source might be. I didn't know. I thought perhaps the patterns were just random. What I discovered was that as I would follow these patterns of light and sound, I would find myself awake to and aware of still other experiences. One experience was that of being calm within my own consciousness. I felt peaceful, benevolent, loving, joyful. This was very intriguing to me because, in my everyday life, I had often been impatient and sometimes communicated with a barbed sense of humor, and I tended to be very active, both physically and mentally. In being attentive to these patterns of light and sound, I began to experience a different part of myself, one that seemed to be apart from the irritations of everyday life and allowed me to see myself as part of a bigger pattern.

I found that my spiritual travels were similar in many ways to travel here on Earth. When you travel physically, you see new sights, you meet new people, and you often experience yourself in a different way as you get to know another culture. I found that traveling in nonphysical dimensions was much the same. I saw and heard new things.[1] During my travels, I sometimes encountered not physical beings as we think of ourselves here, but nonphysical beings of a different consciousness and light and awareness. Sometimes these beings looked much as we do, though they seemed to emanate more light and to be beautiful to a point of near perfection. Sometimes I had the impression that their forms were much less substantial than a physical body but that they assumed a form that appeared much like a physical body so I would be able to relate to them. Sometimes they seemed to be more of a formation of light or energy with a significantly less defined form. I found that I could communicate with these beings, again not in exactly the same way I talk to people verbally, but almost with a kind of mental telepathy. If anything, nonphysical communication with nonphysical beings is often considerably clearer than communication on the physical plane because it is more intuitive, less cluttered and restricted by language. Some of these spiritual beings became my teachers as they assisted me in more intimately knowing their realms—the spiritual dimensions that were their homes.

I found that, as with any journey, there were places I liked and places in which I did not feel comfortable. There seemed to be places that were more negative than others and places that were more filled with Light and peace. I found myself moving, as much as possible, toward those places of Light and peace so I could have an experience of myself that was uplifting, joyful, and transcendent. I found that I really liked feeling peaceful, and with greater experience, I liked it more and more. I found that when I was traveling and exploring these other dimensions, my mind really did leave me alone. My senses—all of my senses—were filled with the new experiences. There was little room for negativity or for worry. At first, I felt some concern that I was tampering with things I should not know. I wondered if I was inviting strange forces into my life and into my awareness. I thought about these things and decided it was important to know my own purpose for this exploration. Was I just after sensation? Was I after power? Was I after an ability to control others or certain situations? What was my *intention?* What was my *purpose?* I thought about these things a great deal.

I realized that if I wanted personal power from these experiences and succeeded in getting it, I would run the risk of being corrupted by the power. If I wanted to control other people, I realized I would set myself up for vengeance once the others realized their own power. If I was just after sensation, I could more easily achieve sensation through various consciousness-altering substances available on the physical level. I realized the only intention that would make this exploration valid for me was the intention to know more of myself and the nature of my soul and, ultimately, to know more of God. I realized it was very important to keep that intention present in my consciousness while I was exploring higher dimensions. I actually felt like something of a scientist— exploring for the sake of exploration, experimenting for the sake of finding out what was present—an explorer for God.

My explorations taught me that the soul is noninflictive. Though it is the most powerful part of our being, it can appear to be the weakest. It is the strongest in that it endures beyond all the other expressions. However, it appears to be the weakest because, here on the physical level, it will give up to other expressions. If you want to express anger, hatred, or jealousy, the soul allows that. It will not force you to be loving. It will not force upon you deeper knowledge of a situation. It will not force upon you a higher perspective. It allows you your expression. But if you turn to the soul, if you turn and choose loving rather than the negative expressions, your strength will be amazing. There is a wonderful story told of a man who survived the concentration camps of World War II in spite of his family and many of his friends being killed. Through it all, he continued to do what he could to be of service, to help others, to hold a positive focus of hope. When he was rescued and in the years since, he has said that early on in his imprisonment, he decided that if they could make him hate, they had won. He knew that if he loved, *he* would win, and there was nothing anyone could do about it. That is the soul. That is the strength of the soul.

WHAT IS YOUR PURPOSE? WHAT IS YOUR INTENTION?

Imagine you are preparing yourself for a long and exciting journey. You know that you will explore new, even unexpected, territories. You will be passing through lands with different customs, different languages, and different modes of communication. You sense, or perhaps even know, that along the way you will encounter many choices, each leading down different roads and presenting additional choices. Of course, you are carrying tools: a map and a guidebook. And you learn how to ask local residents for advice. Yet, perhaps the most important tool is your purpose for the journey. It works much like a compass. It is a steady reference point that brings clarity and sharpness to all your other tools.

Be honest and be present. Be open and loving. Be creative and resourceful. You can approach your journey like a true explorer or even like a scientist. This may be the most exciting journey you have ever taken.

If you would practice Soul Transcendence, reach within yourself with the intention of being in communion with your soul. Go within and practice being attuned to your inner worlds. Practice letting go of your focus on this world and all its glamour and illusion. Look beyond your physical senses to more subtle levels of perception. Follow your breath to a presence deep within you. You are present. And at the same time, you are traveling in your inner awareness. With your purpose at hand, keep choosing the loving, the adventure, the expansion.

Breathe. Allow yourself to rest deeply in the silence of your soul. As you embark on this journey, remember that the soul is not about gain in the world. Your soul

*is about knowing itself more purely, knowing Spirit
and God more completely. Your soul seeks the experience
of its divine nature.*

*If you would know your soul, take time to explore
and practice awareness of the deep inner space where
it resides.*

CHAPTER TWELVE

BREAKING THROUGH TO SOUL — A CELEBRATION

TWELVE

My experience with spiritual exercises expanded and deepened day by day and month by month. I often felt myself to be in a state of pure bliss. Sometimes I thought I had experienced all there was to experience. I often thought I had discovered heaven and did not see how there could be anything more or greater. It seemed that my life here was in perspective. I knew the spiritual worlds were greater than I could ever have imagined and I could spend the rest of my life exploring and growing in these realms. And yet, as time went on, I found that there were even more and higher levels just waiting to be discovered.

One day, as I had traveled into the mental level, I continued to listen for a sound that might lead me onward. Instead I encountered a great silence, an absolute stillness that was new. I wondered if I had gone as far as there was to go. There was a distant pinpoint of light that beckoned me still further. The color of this light was familiar to me. It was the deep purple I had experienced at times when I saw my spiritual teacher in my dreams, the same color I sometimes saw in my meditations. I followed it. I stayed as silent and as focused within my own consciousness as I could. Then, within the silence, I heard the sound of a distant buzzing. Suddenly, my inner vision filled with an immense matrix of shapes and symbols, all vibrating ever so slightly. I saw the chaos of creation, here in the realm of the unconscious. It seemed molten and malleable. Nothing was distinct but, rather, it all appeared as a puzzle, with pieces hidden and magical. It seemed in some ways an endless and empty space, rich in potential but strangely barren in manifestation. And later on, when I had more experience in traveling these levels of consciousness, I would come to know that this region of the unconscious separates all the lower levels (physical, imaginative, emotional, and mental) from the realm of the soul.

The beings I encountered here in the realm of the unconscious were most unusual. They were what I have called "doubles," beings that looked, for example, just like me or just like others I knew in the physical world. They are, in a sense, false images, but they appear quite real. If I related to them as though they were what or who they appeared to be, the result was quite confusing. I had to train myself to become aware of even more subtle energies so I could discern this unconscious level correctly. There were beings, too, who appeared in what seemed akin to Halloween costumes, which were a distortion of something known. It was like a costume that could be discarded at any moment to reveal yet another shape. The images in this dimension are hard to describe. If you think of dreams you may have had that seem to come from your unconscious mind and of some of the strange, conflicting, confusing imagery of those dreams, you'll have the flavor of how images in this unconscious level appear.

On this level, there is also a darkness that is so close and seems so impenetrable that there is almost a sense of vertigo and the urge to turn back to more familiar and comfortable spaces. There is no sign of the magnificence that is on the higher side of this dimension. There is no obvious sign of the soul's perfection. There is little sense of the soul's joy and innocent loving. Darkness pervades this level of the unconscious realm. It was by holding my intention to know the soul that I was able to move past these areas of darkness.

As I traveled the higher realms of light and sound, the sense of spiritual promise grew stronger day by day. My awareness of Spirit, of nonphysical masters and beings, of dimensions beyond the physical world was increasing constantly. And instances of far memory became more frequent. My spiritual exercises and travels were taking me further. I simply continued on. When I could not see beyond the empty space, the void that seemed to fill my consciousness, I continued on. I kept my awareness as open and expanded as possible. I attuned my spiritual vision to whatever might be next. I listened inwardly for what I might hear next. Have you ever been working on, say, a mathematical problem where the answer was unclear to you? You continue to check your figures, you continue to focus on the problem, you continue to look for the answer, and then eventually, it appears to you, and what was not clear becomes clear. My experience was something like that. In my inner consciousness, in my spiritual exercises, I continued to focus on the void, operating with a kind of faith that it would not forever appear to be nothing—and then it shifted in my awareness. The separation of the negative and positive worlds receded, and I continued to evolve upward through this abyss that is the unconscious.

My travels through these spiritual dimensions taught me that the beings on each level are restricted in their movement and in their awareness by their inability to receive and use the energies of Light and Sound above the realm that they are on. It seems to be part of an essential spiritual lesson. If we accept restriction, we manifest restriction. It's true on the physical level, also. If you feel you are not worthy of a great job, a particular salary, or a loving spouse, you create your own restriction. When you believe you are worthy of good things, good things come to you. Believing in yourself is a way you receive and use Spirit's Light energy. On the spiritual levels, too, I experienced that as long as I could keep expanding and supporting my value to receive more of God's Light and Sound, I could keep moving up in these spiritual dimensions. If I became judgmental of myself or my process, I shut the process down and could no longer move my awareness to the higher spiritual realms.

As I reached beyond the unconscious level, I was flooded with the majestic golden Light of pure, positive Spirit, the Light that is more directly of God. It seemed to lift me higher and higher. I knew the most profound loving from deep within me and was filled with incredible joy. It was as if I could hear God's laughter all around me, and His loving embraced and enfolded me completely. I knew I had come home. The sense of radiance was within me as well as all around me. I felt alive in every atom of my being. I felt as though there were no restrictions on my consciousness. It filled every space. I could touch every corner of the universe. My mind remembered the experience I had had as a child, simultaneously fighting and laughing with my best friend. I remembered the laughter welling up inside of me, filling me, protecting me with a kind of divine grace. And, in my far memory, I remembered the oneness with my spiritual teachers. I knew this radiance from many lifetimes and from the beginning of time. I recognized, finally, that I had always been in touch with my soul and divine nature. I had never been separate from it. It had always been present, as the best part of me. It was my laughter, my loving, my enthusiasm, my devotion, and so much more. It was the part of me that I really liked.

As I traveled further through this dimension of the soul, I was filled with the deepest and most profound peace. I felt as though the waters of a gigantic ocean of healing, loving, and compassionate understanding were nourishing and healing me of all the hurts and fears and upsets that had ever occurred on any level, at any time, in any moment of existence. I discovered that the soul is the home of God's word, God's Sound, and God's breath. These images I give you here are metaphors. They are not the experience itself, but I hope they can give you the sense of what I was discovering here in this spiritual dimension and what you can also discover and experience for yourself. The bliss, the peace, the loving, the sense of connection and belonging were nothing like anything I had experienced on Earth. If I took the greatest moment in my life and doubled it and doubled it again and again, I still would not be close. It was magnificent.

I heard the most heavenly singing of angels, thousands of the sweetest tones and voices all together. I heard the sounds of flutes playing their melodies of God. I allowed myself to drink of these celestial melodies. I allowed the healing and the expansion to take place. I welcomed it. I reveled in it. I allowed the clear radiance of the Holy Spirit to wash through me as I looked upward into the God realms above, into the worlds without end. I could see a line of energy stretching upward in the most glorious colors, beyond description in vocabulary, but accessible through the Spirit, through the soul. I could see this line of energy reach on and on, providing me with a lifeline to God, providing me with a lineage, a heritage, and the fulfillment of a promise from God to bring me home and to claim me as His son. I knew that it was a promise made not just to me, but to every soul, to every one of us. I knew that Christ had come to show us the way, to make the way clear. Other great spiritual teachers and masters have done, and continue to do, the same. They assist us to awaken to our own soul, our own connection to God, our own journey home.

I had found my way home to my Father-Mother-God. Like the prodigal son who said, *"Father, I have sinned against heaven and against you. I am no longer worthy to be called your son,"* I didn't feel worthy to receive the abundance of joy and beauty that I discovered here in my spiritual home. In the story, however, nothing is denied to the prodigal son. The father says to his servants, *"Quick! Bring the best robe and put it on him. Put a ring on his finger and sandals on his feet. Bring the fattened calf and kill it. Let's have a feast and celebrate. For this son of mine was dead and is alive again; he was lost and is found."* And even when the older brother was angry and upset that his younger brother was welcomed home without reproach, the father said again, *"We have to celebrate and be glad because this brother of yours was dead and is alive again; he was lost and is found."* In Spirit, I was welcomed home with unconditional joy and loving. I was denied nothing. It was as though I had never left. The perfection from which I had begun my journey was completely present. All the beings and angels of Light, spiritual masters and teachers I had encountered throughout my soul's journey joined in to celebrate my homecoming. I had never known such joy. It was more than I could have ever imagined.

I knew that the high realms of Light and the consciousness of soul were my heritage. I knew I was a child of God and heir to the kingdom. Through what I call the audible Light stream that extends beyond expression into the heart of God, I experienced the divinity that is the spiritual heritage of all mankind. For we are all heirs to God's divinity. We are each made in God's image. No one is separate from this. The Light and Sound come to us through our consciousness of God.

And each one of us chooses whether or not to follow a spiritual path. God has chosen us, and we choose whether or not to choose back to God, whether or not to choose our souls above the world. The soul is always as close as our next breath. It is actually a very simple thing to choose the soul. It is simply a matter of consistently choosing the positive, rather than the negative.

I had discovered that beyond the physical, the imagination, the emotions, the mind, and the unconscious was the soul. I had discovered, at last, the identity of the one who said "my body," "my mind," "my feelings." The soul—which is sacred and has been kept sacred since the beginning and the dawning of time—has remained connected with God and is at one with the spirit of creation. The soul is neutral. It is the holder of the positive energy. The soul's destiny is to learn about itself, about the greater Spirit and God, and to use the knowledge to travel home to the God source.

The soul is gathering experience on this and other levels. Experiencing and accepting are how the soul grows and moves toward greater awareness of God. The soul is masterful at accepting and experiencing whatever is present, whatever is brought forward, whatever is presented—always accepting and experiencing and always without judgment. The soul accepts experience as simply as breathing in and breathing out.

It is through the vehicle of the soul that each one of us entered into the physical earth-plane. It is through the vehicle of the soul that we all shall leave this physical earth-plane. While we are here, we experience this level and accept that which is our experience. The soul is safe and secure here, protected by its divinity. It remains connected to God, to Spirit, to the Light. As we attune to it, we can enhance our sense of divinity and oneness and bring to ourselves greater joy, peace, loving.

My daily practice of spiritual exercises revealed to me that my soul values most those things which reflect its own nature. I see this in other people's expressions, as well as my own. I see that the soul values the awareness of God and Spirit. It values loving, integrity, joy, and peace. It values laughter and the feeling of family, of belonging. It does not value money or cars or houseboats, skis or skateboards, televisions and computers. These are things of the world. They may be tools to accomplish physical goals, and as such, they are useful. But they are not what matters most to the soul in its journey home to God. What matters most is that the soul knows itself and knows God. And that is achieved inwardly.

T HE SOUL IS JOYFUL. *When you are joyful, it's a sure sign that the Spirit is present. The soul stands as the positive polarity, balancing the negative elements of the lower levels. Joy is to be cultivated. It is to be embraced. It is to be celebrated. Take time in your life to be joyful. Do what brings you joy. Joy will lead you toward your soul. It will awaken the soul and allow it to spread its wings and give back to you its positive energy, innocence, and connection to Spirit.*

If you would practice Soul Transcendence, consider joining the celebration. For you are invited! The celebration is present wherever you find joy. Sometimes it bubbles up from within, without any apparent prompting. You may find it in fellowship with others. You can find it in your spontaneous laughter. Go ahead, laugh often. Be silly. Be goofy. Step beyond your inhibitions, your fears of being judged, your illusions of sophistication, and let yourself play in the fields of Spirit and soul. Spirit is not somber and still. It is free and spontaneous. Don't be afraid of the best part of you. Let the you that you like the best shine out in the world. Delight in it. When you are happy, when you are laughing, when you are loving, the radiance of your soul shines through, and all are lifted by it.

Remember, there is a loving and forgiving Father who is waiting to welcome you and celebrate your homecoming.

CHAPTER THIRTEEN

SPIRITUAL EXERCISES – KEYS TO SOUL TRANSCENDENCE

There is a story told that when God created the earth and man, he made a promise to man: "I will reside with my people on Earth. Because the purpose for the creation is for God to know all aspects of Itself in all manifestations (including the negative), there will be negativity on the planet. So I will hide myself in a secret place where the negativity cannot corrupt my spirit."

"I will walk with you," God said to the first man, "and be with you always. I will always be as close to you as your next breath." Man heard the promise and was comforted. And God wondered where that secret place might be, that place that would always be protected from the evil of the world, where God could not be corrupted or tarnished by the world.

At first, God thought He might hide Himself on top of the highest mountain in all the world. But then He thought that man would be sure to find Him there because He knew that man would be ingenious and clever and resourceful. God saw how the first man to discover Him on the mountaintop might exploit his discovery and use it to the disadvantage of others. So then God thought that perhaps

He could hide Himself at the bottom of the deepest ocean. But again, He knew that man's resourcefulness and ingenuity would eventually find Him there and, again, the discovery could be used to the disadvantage of others. Then God had a brilliant idea. He thought He would hide Himself inside of each and every person—not in a physical place but within the spiritual heart of man, in the place of man's loving and compassion. God knew that the last place man would look to find God was within himself. He knew that if man had the ingenuity and the perseverance to seek within, he would value the discovery and keep it safe from those who would corrupt or denigrate it.

Living on the planet Earth and dealing with all the experiences of the planet, people can very easily lose touch with the closeness of God. People have searched for God for eons. And all the time, God has been safely hidden within each and every person.

My spiritual journeys—both inner and outer—continued. I found spiritual teachers who took me higher in awareness. My spiritual exercises took me closer and closer to where God was residing within me. Spiritual exercises revealed to me how greatly the soul yearns to be active, to have expression, and to be acknowledged. One day I went to visit a man who had previously been my teacher. He was talking with his students, and he asked me to come and sit in his chair and talk to his students. I could think of nothing to say. So I said the truth: "There is nothing I can tell you." I saw the room start to get bright as the energy began to shift. I felt the presence of Spirit. And I realized that something more than me was present and that the students were going to have an experience, no matter what I did or did not say. Knowing it didn't matter what I said, I told a joke. It was funny, and everyone laughed uproariously. And I realized I was there to be a joker. My ego would have preferred to have given the students a beautiful message of divinity. But I kept my behavior congruent with my experience, and that was good. I was able to be in sync with what I perceived as the truth of that moment, and I didn't try to control it or make it what it was not.

At another time, my spiritual teacher invited me to answer questions from his students. This time, as the students asked their questions, I answered to the level of my ability to answer. It was simple. I answered from my experience. If I had no experience with what they asked, I simply said I didn't know. I didn't have to be an expert. I could just share what I knew.

The question I heard over and over, in many different words, was, "How do I get in touch with myself? How do I know who I am? Is there something more than the physical body, mind, and emotions? Why do I have to go through heartache, sorrow, suffering, and separation? Why can I not know God and have joy?" It is the question I still hear asked. It's the question we all ask over and over, in so many ways. The answer I knew then is the answer I know today, and it is that you must allow yourself to become quiet enough so that you can hear the stirring of your own soul. There is nothing to *do*. There is nothing outside of yourself to know. You must simply listen to the part of you that says, "I am what I am." That part will not think. It will not feel. It will not have a body. It will not wear any coat or covering. It is what it is, nothing more, nothing less. It is divine. It is the spark of God. It is who you truly are, on this level and on all the other levels. It is the soul.

We all experience the soul from time to time. Most of us don't know what the soul is and have not been taught how to recognize it, so we tend to miss it. Some qualities of the soul are joy, love, enthusiasm, freedom, and peace. You have felt the movement of your soul. Let me suggest to you some of the moments when you may have felt the stirring of your soul. You may have felt the stirring of your soul on your wedding day, in the moment when you and the one you love came together in the presence of family and friends to pledge your love for one another. There may have been a

moment when you experienced a pure love, a sense of perfection, boundless hope, and a promise of joy like you had
never known before. Or you may have attended a wedding
where you experienced the bride and groom at such a
moment. You may have found yourself crying just a little bit
because something of the loving and the beauty touched you
and stirred and moved your soul. Sometimes, you don't
know why you cry at weddings, but there is a certain feeling
that you catch and it resonates inside of you. Your soul may
respond, and for a moment, you also experience the loving,
the hope, the joy, and the renewal.

Do you know what we so often say when we fall in
love? "I couldn't help myself." And it's true. In that
moment, when the soul sees a reflection of itself in another,
when it sees loving, beauty, hope, joy, it cannot help but
respond. It cannot help but reach out for the experience
of loving. The awakening of the soul often starts when the
soul sees itself in someone else. The awakening can begin
when you meet a spiritual leader who is awake to his or
her own soul—and yours. The awakening can begin in its own
timing when you hear within yourself God's question,
"When are you coming home?"

Sometimes when a new mother or father looks at their
baby, they experience their souls awakening, stirring.

Their souls see something precious in their child that is not quite of this earth. Their souls glimpse eternity in that baby and respond with joy. Mothers and fathers typically fall madly in love with their children. Often it is a love that transcends all other kinds of earthly love. There is purity with it and an unconditional quality that is truly of the soul and of God. A parent's love for their child may come closest to the way God loves each of us unconditionally.

Another of life's experiences that often calls forward this heightened awareness of the soul is when a loved one is close to death. When a person nears the moment when he or she will be leaving this physical earth, the soul becomes more active, more present as it prepares for the next step in its journey. And everyone who is close is touched by a magical sense of being in a timeless space. So many of the normal earthly concerns fade away, and it can be as if the essence of each person is entirely present for the other. Awarenesses are heightened. People find the courage to say what may not have been said for a lifetime. Hurt feelings fade away in the face of things far more important. The essence of loving may come present, sweeping everything else away. Sometimes the one who is dying has transcendent experiences. They may see light or feel themselves moving toward the Light. They may hear violins or other music or sounds. Many times, they mention the beauty they are seeing "on the other side" and the peace they are feeling. People who are near them and loving them are touched by the closeness of the soul, and it stirs and awakens their own souls within.

These are all very powerful experiences, ones you never forget. Perhaps you have had experiences like these or others that were transcendental, experiences that gave you a glimpse of something in yourself greater than what you are normally aware of in your everyday life.

I think it's clear that there is more to this experience we call life than going to work and paying the bills, doing the dishes, and getting the kids off to school. I think we know that we are something more than our personalities and our egos, our emotions and our bodies. I think it's obvious to nearly everyone that there is more, because I think that "more" is part of everyone's experience—somehow and in some way. And I think that most of us long for the "more" we only experience from time to time. I think we long to be in love and to experience the heightened awareness and aliveness that "being in love" brings us. I think we long to experience the joy we had when we watched a son or daughter take their first steps, the loving we experience for that very special person, the sweetness of our family's love and support as we complete something important to us, the sense of "all's right with the world" we experience from time to time on a perfect spring morning when, for some reason, everything falls into place and it all seems perfect. We have those experiences every now and then, though we don't seem to have them every day. They often seem elusive, distant, and unattainable. Perhaps they seem that way only because we do not give them our daily focus and attention. I believe spiritual exercises are the key to finding more of the soul experience in everyday life. It has certainly been my key to soul awareness.

The soul is our truest essence. It's the divinity in you, in me, in everyone. When it stirs, there is a brief glimpse of something more than the physical reality, a sense of presence, a sense of Spirit. Sometimes the energy of that is so strong you can ride on it for years. My spiritual teachers had experienced their divinity. They were awakened to their souls. It was what they sought to teach me and others. But it's really impossible to teach about the soul because the sense of it almost has to be caught, not learned. That's why spiritual teachers often seem to talk nonsense. They are trying to communicate, to impart something about an essence that is beyond words, beyond thought, beyond the senses of this world.

JOHN-ROGER HAS SHARED MANY CLUES *for how you can experience your soul and how to increase your awareness of the soul. There are words he repeats when he talks about the soul, words like* loving, joy, innocence, kindness, freedom, peace, and gratitude. *They point our way toward the soul. He has talked about the importance of using his intention to keep going and being clear about his purpose for exploring Soul Transcendence. And he has described the techniques he has used to make his explorations more methodical, practical, and workable for himself and others.*

You may find it useful to create a personal journal to record your experiences of soul. Use it to note the methods and approaches that are working for you in your journey back home. Make it a record of your moments of transcendence, loving, and joy. Use it as inspiration when you are feeling discouraged or down, or just to lift you higher.

Write your prayers in it. Write letters to your soul. Perhaps you'll fill it with drawings your children give you, cards from loved ones, and pictures you treasure. It can be a journal for your soul, and it will help awaken you to the moments when you know your soul in its beauty and radiance.

You may begin to practice spiritual exercises, taking time to be quiet, to reach beyond the confines of your physical body, mind, and emotions and to find out what lies beyond. You may pray or meditate or read inspirational works. You might listen to the CD enclosed in this book, Inner Journey Through Spirit Realms.[2]

If you would practice Soul Transcendence, explore ways you can exercise your awareness of soul and Spirit. Spiritual exercises, in their many forms, are keys that unlock doors into the experience of the soul.

CHAPTER FOURTEEN

SAYING YES TO SOUL AND SERVICE

FOURTEEN

Is it possible that when God created mankind, He intended us to have joy and to have it more abundantly than most of us have ever dreamed possible? I think the answer is *yes*. If we have a spark of the divine within us, if we are of God, then are not all things possible? Again, I think the answer is yes. So the question becomes, how can we consciously awaken the soul inside of us so that we can, at will, tap in to that strange, wonderful, alive feeling—that sense of transcendence, of belonging to God and not to this earth?

My spiritual exercises continued to reveal to me patterns of cause and effect that had heretofore been obscure. My travels into other dimensions were filled with new aware-nesses. So many questions about the universe, about mankind, about myself, and about others were answered almost before I knew to ask them. Teachers on this physical level provided me with wisdom and experiences that matched the teachings provided to me on inner levels and through my far memories.

I came to know the qualities of Light and Sound in the spiritual dimensions because they were tangible there. I could see the spiritual Light there. The beings I saw on my spiritual travels *were* Light, and they emanated Light. I realized that here on the physical planet, we reflect light. It does not come from within. In the spiritual dimensions, the Light comes from within. I could hear the Sound of Spirit on the other levels, and I could bring that Sound into myself and resonate to that Sound. I realized that when it says in the Bible, "In the beginning was the Word," the Word is the Sound of God. It is a basic element of creation. Light is another basic element of creation.

The Light and the Sound are also present on the physical level, though they tend to be harder to distinguish here because there is so much light of a coarser nature and there is so much sound that is more brash and strident. The Light and Sound of God are quite subtle here so they are easy to miss. But if you sit and become very, very quiet you will see Light and hear Sound of a quality that is not of this earth. Many Eastern spiritual groups seek to experience the Light and the Sound in their meditations. In Psalm 23 in the Bible (King James version), there is a verse: "Thy rod and thy staff, they comfort me." I believe these are references to the Sound and the Light. Rod and staff. Sound and Light.

As I practiced my spiritual exercises, I not only traveled into other dimensions and sought to become aware of other levels, I also practiced bringing the Light and the Sound more into this physical world. I practiced bringing the Light and Sound into my body to see what the result would be. As I did this, I found it was easier to be loving, calm, peaceful, and centered. I learned to send the Light ahead of me when I was driving my car, and I could feel a greater level of protection in the world. I learned to send the Light ahead to any and all activities in my day. One thing I found crucial was to always send the Light *for the highest good of all*. The Light, as I've said, is a very powerful tool and it is a spiritual tool. It cannot be used for manipulation or for personal gain. Using it "to get my own way" would only backfire and cause distress. Using it "for the highest good" reminded me that the Spirit knows what is best in a way greater than I, from the physical level, could ever hope to know. These tools of Spirit will not be abused. We can abuse and misuse tools of the world and try to manipulate them to our own seeming advantage. We cannot abuse the Light and Sound of Spirit. To try will set us back in many ways.

I learned that I could ask for the Light to be present in a physical location and that it would assist in bringing balance to that location. It was not unlike what I saw when traveling in the spiritual dimensions, when I saw healing come to the Earth as it was surrounded in beautiful emerald green light.

I found that placing Light in certain areas was more effective when I was physically present. It seemed important to take the awareness of the Light to certain places at certain times, and to that end, I spent some time traveling physically throughout the United States to do this type of work.

One night, I stopped in a little Midwestern town. I had driven most of the day and was looking forward to getting some dinner and then some rest. I took a good pair of pants out of my bag, to wear that night for dinner, and a travel steamer to get the wrinkles out. I sat down on the side of the bed to wait for the steamer to warm up. As I was sitting there, the lights in the room seemed to start flickering, or perhaps something from outside was flicking light around the room. Whatever it was, it was unusual. At first I thought it might be car lights from outside, and then I realized the windows in the room were on an inner court, so that couldn't be it. Then I thought perhaps it was from other people opening or closing nearby doors, but I realized that there wasn't enough activity in the courtyard for it to be that. So I decided to ignore it. I put my head down to focus on steaming my pants, and all of a sudden, I had the strangest sensation all through my body. As I glanced up, I saw a most unusual Light formation appear over the door. I thought my eyes were tired and playing tricks on me. What I was seeing was a shimmering image of a figure beginning to form. That one area of the room by the door was flickering and shimmering with Light. And I could feel an energy, a presence that was more than flickering patterns of light. I was mesmerized. This was akin to experiences I'd had on spiritual dimensions, but I had never before had this kind of experience on the physical level, in daylight, with my eyes open.

Then suddenly, the shimmering, flickering light became a more defined shape as it began to form itself into a more substantial image of a man who then appeared to be standing just inside the doorway. He was magnificent beyond all my powers to describe him. He was radiant, bright and Light, and he emanated a tremendous power. The air felt charged, alive, and sparkling with a pulsating energy. I was dumbstruck. I was in awe and found I was shaking. I wasn't sure who or what he was. But I did not sense danger. I was not afraid. There was no sense at all of malevolence. I knew there were magnificent beings of Spirit that existed on the other, non-physical realms but I had never entertained that one might materialize in a simple hotel room in the Midwest. I felt so humble that such a one as this should appear before me. He started moving toward me, and I saw that he was floating, not walking, through the space. As soon as I noticed that and my awareness formed the thought, his feet settled gently down to earth. With that, I realized he knew my thoughts. I knew there was no separation between us. He reached toward me and put his hands on my head, and for a few minutes, I thought my head was going to explode. It was unbearable. It was excruciating. It was wonderful. It seemed that all the energy flooding through this being was pouring into my head. It was more than I could bear, and yet I could have borne it forevermore.

He did not speak in words, but he told me of things I could do to bring greater spiritual energy to the physical earth-plane and to the people of the Earth. He showed me how I could be of service to the greater good of men and women everywhere. He showed me what my work on Earth would be, how I could share my own experience with others and assist them in awakening themselves to Spirit and to their own divinity. As I was shown the possibilities and the potentials, there was also the question presented: Was I willing to do these things? Was I willing to set aside my personal concerns and goals and walk this new path opening before me?

In my heart, I said yes to everything. My answer was never in doubt. As he communicated with me, all my fear left me. All my considerations dissolved. I saw my way clearly. From where I was, it looked easy. All I said was yes. It wasn't dramatic. It didn't feel like any big deal. It was very simple. And it changed my life forever. As my soul—which I knew then to be the essence of my being—embraced this magnificent being of Light, his message, his direction, and his brotherhood, he turned and began to move back toward the door and then was gone. In that moment, as he disappeared, I was overcome with an immediate and irresistible sleepiness. Even today, I am not sure whether I saw him vanish before I was asleep or if I fell asleep as he moved away. Either way, I just toppled over where I was and was asleep in an instant.

The next morning, I woke up just where I had fallen asleep, slumped sort of sideways over the bed. At first, I didn't remember anything of the night's events. I wondered why my shorts and shirt were all wrinkled and why I looked like such a mess. I realized I must have fallen asleep and knew I'd missed dinner. And then I remembered this wondrous being of Light who had appeared to me. I remembered the communication. I remembered I had said an unequivocal *yes* to all of his requests. I didn't know whether to think of the implications of his visit—or think about the steamer I knew I had not turned off. Inevitably, I thought about the steamer first (physical habits are tenacious) and discovered it lying by the bed, cold, so I thought it likely that I'd burned out the motor. I stood up and started to get organized for the day, when suddenly the steamer started to hiss and steam. A sign that the events of the night before were not my imagination? Coincidence? I didn't know.

Gradually, I began to think about my experience, of the shimmering lights, the radiant Light being, his message, and the commitment I'd made. A part of me thought I'd had a most incredible spiritual experience, and my mind—being my mind—still wondered if I was hallucinating or if I had perhaps dreamed these things. Deep inside of me, however, my heart and my soul were experiencing something much more than a hallucination or a dream could have elicited. There was a change happening within me. There was an even greater awakening. I could sense it. I could feel it. There was a dawning sense of realization and awareness that there was so much more to this world and this universe than I had ever imagined. I realized that even the spiritual experiences I'd had up to this point were, perhaps, just a beginning. It seemed likely that there was going to be much more.

The night before had provided me with an encounter with a magnificent, radiant, majestic spiritual being. The morning brought doubt, confusion, exhilaration, certainty, change, and a level of mundane, everyday reality. So it was in this state of confusion and clarity that I set out for the next town, the next stop in my summer's journey through the heartland of America. It was raining hard and I had to drive slowly. I had a speaking engagement that evening in a town hundreds of miles away, and at this rate, I wasn't at all sure I could make it on time. I was also feeling very tired and wasn't sure I could stay awake to drive straight through without stopping. It occurred to me that if I could get someone to drive the car, it would help a lot. I was on the freeway. It was raining. I saw a man standing under an overpass. I hoped he was hitchhiking and not waiting for a bus. When I got closer, I could see he was thumbing, so I pulled right over and stopped. He opened the door, and the first thing I said to him was, "Do you know how to drive?" He said he did, and I said, "Well, come on and drive." He walked around to the driver's side and got in as I slid over. I said, "I'm so glad you're here because I'm so tired." With no more ado than that, I told him where I was going, which he said was near his own destination. I said, "You're just heaven sent." And then I happened to look down at his shoes, which were black and shiny and dry. I looked at his clothes, and they were dry, too. I thought that was strange, considering the downpour outside, but I wasn't going to ask him any questions because all I wanted to do was get some sleep.

When I woke up, the sun was shining, the skies were clear, and I was feeling refreshed and renewed. My hitchhiker said,

"I'm going to be getting out before we reach the city," and in just a few moments, he stopped the car, got out, and waved goodbye. I realized we were very close to the city where I was scheduled to speak that evening. I looked at my watch—which turned out to be confusing and made me wonder if we'd gone through a time change or something. Then I looked at my odometer and realized that if it and my watch were both accurate, we had gone about 350 miles in three to four hours. I wondered if he had stopped for gas and thought I'd ask. But when I looked for him, he wasn't there. I got out and looked down the road and up the road. All I saw were fields of wheat stubble. I got on top of the car and looked for him with my binoculars, but no one was anywhere in sight. I backed my car down the road about a hundred yards. Though the road was muddy, there were no footprints. There were no tracks. There was nothing that would indicate a man had been there. And I thought about his shiny black shoes and dry clothes and wondered.

I drove into the city and arrived in plenty of time for my evening engagement. I thought about all the events of the preceding twenty-four hours. I knew I was seeing, manifested in the physical world, a transference of things I had been experiencing on other levels in higher worlds. The spirit, the Light, the loving, the connectedness I experienced in nonphysical dimensions were not separate from this level. What did this mean to me? And what was it that I had really said *yes* to, in my reply to the spiritual form that appeared to me? As best I could describe it then, it meant a commitment—not only to my own journey home to God but to assist others in their journey home to God in whatever way I could. It meant sharing my experiences with others. It meant sharing the truth as I saw it with others. It meant loving people—all people—to my greatest capacity. It meant letting go of excuses for holding back my loving. It meant going beyond the excuses of "I'm too tired" or "I don't have time" or "I can't do that" or "I'll look foolish" if there was an opportunity to help. It meant being true to myself, to my soul, to the Spirit, and to God as I knew it. It meant unconditional loving. A part of me was elated. A part of me was really scared.

I F YOU WOULD PRACTICE SOUL
TRANSCENDENCE, *be open to Spirit showing*
up in your life. You never know the form it will take.
Sometimes it takes the form of your husband or wife.
Sometimes it takes the form of your boss or best friend.
And sometimes it takes a supernatural form that is
unmistakably not of this Earth. There are masters and
angels of Light that share physical space with us. We
don't often see them. If we pay attention, we may be
able to sense their presence.

You can cultivate the presence of Spirit in your life by
focusing your awareness on the Light of the Holy Spirit
and by using the Light in your daily life. Take time to
pray every day for the Light to surround, fill, and protect
you. It's a good idea to ask "for the highest good." This
way, you are aligning yourself with God's will rather than
your own limited perspective. Send the Light to your family,

those you love, your community, and the world. Send Light to difficult situations. Ask Spirit to assist you in everything you do. Make the Light and God your partners.

If you would know your soul, practice being in service to the higher Spirit. And when you are guided by the Light to do those things that are uplifting, hopeful, helpful, say yes. When Spirit asks you to extend kindness and consideration to another human being, say yes. When you have the opportunity to experience the depth of your soul, say yes. Say yes to your soul and it will guide you home.

If you would know Soul Transcendence, be willing to serve.

CHAPTER FIFTEEN

GUIDING THE WAY HOME

FIFTEEN

It had become irrefutable that there was a great deal more to the universe than I or anyone could perceive with just the physical senses, that there were spiritual dimensions transcending the earth plane. Experiences from my childhood supported this idea, and certainly, experiences I was having as an adult supported it. Spiritual exercises supported this. Seeing beings from other dimensions materialize on this level brought it into much sharper focus. There was tremendous support for spiritual ideas and ideals in literature and stories from all cultures, from all times, from all people. Many of the best minds that mankind has produced have argued for the existence of God or a supreme being of some kind. And of course, there are the Bible, the Koran, the Bhagavad Gita, and other great books and stories of great masters and the miracles they performed—all of which tell stories of Spirit, of Light, of God. In the Western world, we tend to think that great spiritual events occurred in the past and are not part of present-day reality. And even if they could occur today, we doubt they could occur to ordinary people. But what if this is not true? What if each person—right here, right now, today—is a divine being? What if the soul that resides deep within each person can awaken and realize itself and its own nature? What if the abilities of the Christ and Buddha and Mohammed and other great masters are not just myths and stories but tell of a greater reality that is as available today as it was in ancient times? What if the reality of God is the same today as ever? My experiences of Spirit opened my eyes to many possibilities of what could take place here. It opened my eyes to the possibilities that are available to everyone who chooses the higher path, who chooses the soul. All that has ever been available through Spirit to mankind is available right now to everyone. We are never separate from our divine nature. We can pretend otherwise, but we can claim our spiritual heritage at any moment and turn our feet toward home.

I found that, as I was traveling more on the spiritual levels and learning more about Spirit and God, I was feeling less and less connection to what I was doing in my physical life, in terms of what I did to earn a living. I found that the routines I had established before what you might call my spiritual awakening were not as relevant as they had seemed before. And yet, there was a certain amount of familiarity with what I was doing physically, the routines of my life. There was a sense of comfort and security. Part of it was money and financial security, but part of it was also a certain identity, certain associates and colleagues, and a certain expertise at my job. But I knew this was not all I was to do with my life. I knew I must move on and do other things in this world. I knew that the promises I made that night to the being of Light could not be ignored. A part of me wanted to reach out and embrace the new—new challenges, opportunities, and possibilities. And a part of me wanted to stay with the comfort and security of the old.

For a while, I tried to blend the two and make it work that way. I tried to claim the new without giving up the old. That didn't work very well. I was becoming more and more dissatisfied with the old, and I was beginning to know I would have to let go of my old life patterns and old ways before I could fully claim the new.

I began to look at the price I would have to pay to get out of where I was, to get out of what I was doing in order to create the freedom to move into the new work that was clearly part of my spiritual promise and my soul's destiny. I didn't know what the price might be. I wondered if I might be poor or unable to earn a living. I wondered if I would be ostracized by former colleagues. I wondered what my family would think. I wondered what my friends would think. I wondered if they would call me names or not invite me to anything ever again. I didn't know what the price would be. And for a time, I was unwilling to find out.

But the sense of purpose kept growing and growing inside of me until it became impossible to ignore. I realized that this was something I was going to do, no matter what the price. I realized the Spirit was coming so alive inside of me, the experiences my soul was bringing forward were becoming so powerful and dynamic, and my promise to those in the spiritual realms was so compelling that the concerns of this world were fading by comparison. Even if the price were that I would be cast out and spat upon, or even if the price were death, I knew I would leave what I had been doing on this Earth and begin to teach of the soul, the spirit of man, the Spirit of God, the Light that we all are. I knew it was my destiny. I could not deny it or push it away anymore. In many ways, I had "come home" to God on this physical level, as well as on the spiritual levels.

As I practiced spiritual exercises, I experienced a sense of profound peace, well-being, and contentment that often accompanies "coming home." Present with me nearly all the time was an expanded, joyful sense of belonging to God. It was available to me whenever I focused on it. In my spiritual travels, I regularly allowed myself to drift upward to that realm of the soul where Light and loving are a tangible reality and the sweet Sounds of Spirit fill all awareness. I did, indeed, feel that, after eons of separation and loneliness, I had come home. And through my commitment to the great Spirit, I knew I had the opportunity to assist others in finding their way home to the spirit within themselves, to their souls, to their divine Source.

I had never talked very much to anyone about any of my experiences on any level, and certainly not on the spiritual levels. I had kept my own counsel and was content to gain the knowledge and experience as part of my own growth and expansion. These were sacred spaces to me, sacred experiences. How was I going to share about them? What was I going to share? Who would believe me? Who would be interested? Would I survive the scrutiny of others? Would my experiences prove true? Would I be ridiculed? The answers to all those questions really didn't matter. I realized that I was going to be involved in the process, no matter what the outcome.

"Ground point zero" is the area immediately below the point where a nuclear bomb detonates, the point where everything vaporizes. I knew I might be facing a personal ground point zero: the possible destruction of all that had been constant and secure in my life. "Ground point zero" is how I came to think of this point of change, this point of abandoning all my considerations and natural caution and following Spirit into an entirely new adventure.

To experience my own particular ground point zero, I had to look at what price I was willing to pay. I found the only "coin" I was not willing to pay was my spiritual life, because that is *me*. I wasn't willing to cut my heart out, so to speak, because that's *me*. I wasn't willing to hurt myself, because that's *me*. But I was willing to get rid of everything else, by walking away from it, running if I had to, escaping if that was how it looked. I really didn't care. I didn't care what it looked like. I didn't care what people said or thought. I didn't care if I looked like a fool. I didn't care if it didn't work out in worldly terms. I didn't care what kind of impression I made. Those were an easy price to pay.

When I realized that I was willing to experience ground point zero, when I became willing to let all that had been in my life "vaporize" if necessary, it was amazing how quickly things turned around for me. The way opened for me to leave, within a couple of months, the job that I had been trying to leave for several years. When I left, I decided that I would approach it as though that part of my life were entirely ended. It would be as though I had no job, no career, no money, no family, no girlfriend, no car, no house, no nothing. All was obliterated. All was gone. It was as if a nuclear bomb had gone off in my life and taken out all that was old, all that was from the past, all that was part of my captivity in the illusions of the world.

What happened when I walked away from my job, my former life, my colleagues, my security, my routine, and my so-called responsibilities? I felt free. I didn't have to meet the deadlines of other people. I became my own man, which was really fun. My thinking was not dependent on someone agreeing with me. My feelings did not depend on someone supporting or approving of them. I felt new and clear inside of myself as a spiritual being. Nuclear.

The sense of new and clear—the sense of freedom, the sense of being my own man, the sense of my own soul—was so powerful that it absolutely radiated out from me. I was ready to go out and explode with the dynamics that started coming present in me as a spiritual being. From my own personal ground point zero of blasting away the old and embracing the new, I became full of "nuclear radiation" (new, clear energy/force). Literally, people would stop me on the street and ask what I did. People saw a freedom, a clarity, and a simplicity. People saw the soul because, in my decision to be my own man, I chose for my soul. I allowed the energy of the soul to come more into my physical expression. And the soul in every person, when it sees the soul in another, responds and reaches for that Light, that truth, that radiance. Life is very simple when all the extraneous elements are blasted away and all that is left is a simple person, living simply and focusing on communion with Spirit. There is nothing more simple. Easy? Not necessarily. But definitely simple.

As I opened up to what lay on the other side of the ground-point-zero blast, I found that some people had survived the blast and were still with me, in loving and in freedom. The people who were important in terms of the spiritual energy fields and in terms of the work that I would be doing spiritually didn't even get shaken up by the blast. They actually seemed happy about it and rejoiced that I had moved into what was truly to be mine. They were happy that I had more time and energy to devote to the spiritual work, and they were there in support of the spiritual work I was doing. I also discovered that when I had this "new clear" radiation present and radiating out from me, others who were in that same place—or close to it—were drawn to me, and vice versa. We found one another. We came together and talked about our experiences.

I found that people were experiencing their own versions of ground point zero. One man told me that he was separated from his wife and had recently become romantically involved with a new woman, but he also thought from time to time about reconciling with his wife. So he was experiencing lots of confusion and was not at all sure what he should do. I told him he could do whatever he wanted to do, but there would be a price to pay. It might be hurting his girlfriend's feelings; it might be hurting his wife's feelings. It might be paying alimony. It might be disappointing his family. It might be a lot of things, but he had to look at the consequences, look at the price, and decide if he was willing to pay the price for staying true to himself, whatever that turned out to be. He didn't like to hear there would be a price to pay no matter what his choice, but that was the truth.

When I talked with him about all of this, I remembered and allowed myself to become attuned to the realm I had visited so often, where cause and effect were so clearly part of the whole action. I remembered that karmic law allows each person to bring a completion and a balance to all the actions of their life. I remembered the beings of this dimension and how they were filled with so much acceptance and loving and how the sense of balance was welcomed and embraced. That was the vision I held within my consciousness while this man looked at his choices and decided for the one that held the most loving, truth, and integrity for him. When I saw him choose for his own soul, there was great rejoicing inside of me. And I realized I was finding my next level of vocation: holding a focus of spiritual energy while others came into their own expression of truth and integrity and began to awaken to their own soul.

Later on, I met another man who was in the process of coming to his own ground point zero. For many years, he had been in a marriage that was not nurturing to him, and he didn't seem to have the skills to change it. Over time, he had become impotent with his wife and then had begun to cheat on the marriage to prove that it was not his fault but his wife's. In this process of cheating, he had separated from his family even more, had pulled all his energy back inside of himself, and, in essence, shut himself off. This had a somewhat negative effect on his family, but it had a devastating effect on him. He developed ulcers, back problems, headaches, and even his eyesight was affected. What had happened was that he had shut himself off from his own soul and from his awareness of Spirit within himself and others. He felt isolated, separated, unable to receive help, cast out. He could see no way out. He could see no way to be happy.

He came to me one day and asked if it was spiritually clear for him to kill himself. I thought of all the resources available to him, though he did not know them. I thought of the resources of imagination, how he could use imagery to give himself a new vision of success and joy. I thought of the resources of emotion available to him, where he could begin to manifest the loving that he so desperately wanted. I thought of the resources of the mind, where he could use his intelligence to create new behaviors for himself. And I thought of his soul, wanting to experience connection, oneness, loving, and joy. I told him it was not spiritually clear to kill himself; there was much available to him and much that he could do to "blast" through the illusions of the situation and gain clarity. He said the situation, as it was, was intolerable. I suggested that he change his attitude. He didn't know how, which was obvious or he would have done it sooner.

So I sat with him, and we talked about what he would do in his life if he felt unfettered by wife and family (new imagery). He already had some really clear plans. We talked about what he would do professionally, how he could build a career that was exciting and fulfilling to him—and financially rewarding (new ideas). He had thought of a plan of what to do but he had all the reasons why he couldn't do it: his wife wouldn't let him, he couldn't quit his present job, he didn't have the necessary credentials, not enough money, etc. We talked about how he would feel about himself if he could do the things he'd like to do (new emotions) and how he could use these feelings to support and nurture himself to fulfill even more of what he might be here to do.

We talked about how, if he were willing to let go of having other people's (particularly his wife's and family's) approval, he might well be able to do what he envisioned. So he decided he could do that, and he formulated his plan in detail, set about taking the steps necessary to complete it, and he did it. He changed careers, moved into a whole new field, and became quite successful. When we initially talked about his plans for change, it had seemed to include divorcing his wife and taking some new steps in terms of his personal life. A few years later, after he had changed careers and achieved professional success, he was still with his wife, so I asked him what had happened to change his mind about the divorce. He said that once he realized that he could go for success on his own terms, in the way that he intuitively knew was right for him, he did not need to divorce.

He said, "I told myself that if I didn't have my wife and kids, I could do it this way—and then I did it that way—and what I found out was that I didn't need to divorce my wife at all. I realized that I loved her and I loved my kids, and I really did want to be a family with them." He went to his ground point zero; he experienced the "blast," which signified that he was willing to let go of whatever was holding him back, whatever was in his way, in order to fulfill himself in his own life. And his family survived the blast.

The old was gone, the new was manifested, and everyone was happier.

When you set out on a conscious path of spiritual awakening—by whatever name you call it—it is important to place that first in your life. That protects your integrity with yourself. It means that you will not sell yourself out to accommodate someone else, you will not be coerced into doing things that conflict with your sense of honesty, and you will not make yourself subservient to someone else. It means you stand in a place of responsibility to yourself and your own spirit and soul, no matter what. Does that mean you have to be alone? No. Does it mean that you have to leave your family behind? No. Does it mean you have to quit your job? No. Do you have to be willing to? Yes. Yes, you have to be willing to be aware of what is important to you, what is necessary to you for your next step—and to do that, no matter what.

Each person has his or her own reality. No one can judge from the outside what another person is experiencing or expressing. That is why it is so important for each person to find their own truth, to find what is so for them, because it is always individual. Individual reality is based on many things from the past and from the present. It is based on the experience of the soul and what each individual has learned from their own soul's experience. Ultimately, we live our lives based upon our own experiences, not on someone else's. We may accept someone else's experience or point of view for a time, but eventually, we come face to face with ourselves and what we have learned from our own life.

To those people who are on a conscious spiritual path, it becomes important to face the reality of the situations you created because it is through seeing the face of suffering, despair, joy, heartache, happiness, love—both in yourself and in others—that you see the face of God. The face of God is in everything you experience. The face of God is never hidden from you. You only hide it from yourself when you do not look at what is so, when you do not look at reality, when you pretend that you can make some ideal of yours supersede what reality is. It's a fool's game. Many people do it for long, long periods of time. I did it for eons. When I came to ground point zero, I demonstrated my learning that it does not work to live life from someone else's premise. In order to grow, in order to become your own man or your own woman, you must live life on your own terms. Those terms may not be in conflict with anyone's. Those terms may blend beautifully with your family, your church, your community, and your country. That's fortunate and a great blessing. And if they do not and you choose to walk your own path, that is also fortunate and a great blessing.

All things are of God. Each one of us is a child of God. There is no one outside of God. We each carry a divine spark of energy, the soul, which is a direct extension of God. How we relate to the soul, how we express the soul, how we embrace it or ignore it are our personal choices. There is no right or wrong way to do this. There is no better or worse way to do this. There are many, many choices, and all choices have their consequences. God loves us all, no matter what. God is our Father and our Mother. God is the original unconditional lover of His children, no matter how far they have roamed, no matter what they have done or not done, no matter how separated or alienated they have become. The door is always open. You are always welcome. You can always come home.

If you want to experience more of your own soul, if you want to come home, perhaps my story will give you some new ideas of what you might do. I hope that I've at least pro-voked you to think about your soul and your relationship with the great Spirit of God. God has given each of us the precious gift of life and awareness and then the additional gift of freedom to do with it what we will. God has chosen each one of us as heirs to His kingdom; it's up to us when we choose to return home to Him and claim all that our her-itage offers to us.

If I had a prayer, it would be that each and every one would choose back and come home to God. It has been my choice. I recommend it.

Good journey to you all.

If you would learn the secret of Soul Transcendence,
look only for the good,
for the divine in people and things,
and all the rest, leave to God.

—JOHN-ROGER

NOTES

1. For a pictorial depiction of the realms of spirit, see the Chart of the Realms on page 264.

2. For more information on spiritual exercises and Soul Transcendence as presented by John-Roger, refer to the study materials listed at the end of this book.

CHART OF THE REALMS

REALM	SOUND	COLOR
POSTIVE REALMS		
(Spirit)	(Not Verbalized)	(Not Verbalized)
(Spiritual Light)		
GOD		
27 Levels	HU	
	Thousand violins	
	Angels singing	Clear
	Summer breeze through	Pale Gold
	the willow trees	Light Gold
SOUL	Haunting flutelike sound	Gold
NEGATIVE REALMS	*Cosmic Mirror*	
(Reembodiment levels)		
(Magnetic Light)		
(Karmic Board)		
ETHERIC	Buzzing Bee or	Purple
(Unconscious)	buzzing fly	
MENTAL	Running water or	Blue
(Mind)	babbling brook	
CAUSAL	Tinkling bells	Orange
(Emotions)		
(Karma)		
ASTRAL	Surf/waves	Pink
(Imagination)		
PHYSICAL		
(Conscious self)		
(Physical body)	Thunder; heart beat	Green

Rukmini canal (diagonal text between positive and negative realms)

Subconscious
Unconscious
Habits
Addictions
Obsessions
Compulsions

(Note: High selves and basic selves may come from any level.)

EPILOGUE

It has been my good fortune and my pleasure to have worked with people throughout the world for nearly forty years, assisting them in awakening to their souls and Spirit. If you feel drawn to learn more of this path that I have called Soul Transcendence, you are welcome to contact The Movement of Spiritual Inner Awareness (MSIA) at P.O. Box 513935, Los Angeles, CA 90051-1935. You can also go to this web site: www.msia.org. MSIA offers a variety of programs, books, audiotapes and videotapes.

He that dwelleth in love, dwelleth in God and God in him.

1 John 4:16
(King James Version)

*J*ohn-Roger's teachings are found in a rich variety of materials presented by The Movement of Spiritual Inner Awareness. Here is a brief list of materials you may find helpful in your further exploration of Soul Transcendence.

BOOKS

Momentum: Letting Love Lead—The simplicity of the book's approach communicates a profound message: You can live a fulfilling life, not by trying harder, working more, or sleeping less, but by letting love lead you.
(ISBN 1893020185, Cloth, $19.95)

Spiritual Exercises—Walking with the Lord—An uplifting set of excerpts ranging from "how-to" instructions to inspiring encouragement in reaching into soul via spiritual exercises.
(ISBN 0914829300, Paper, $12)

Inner Worlds of Meditation—A set of specific techniques, each presenting a spiritual exercise focused on a different aspect of Light and Sound.
(ISBN 0914829459, Paper, $12)

Spiritual Warrior—A practical guide to finding greater meaning in everyday life, this revolutionary approach puts us firmly on the higher road to health, wealth, and happiness, prosperity, abundance, and riches, loving, caring, sharing, and touching.
(ISBN 091482936X, Cloth, $20)

Passage Into Spirit—A comprehensive, detailed book dealing with topics including why we are here, the process of incarnation, divine destiny and free will, and the sights and sounds of the five spiritual realms.
(ISBN 0914829254, Paper, $7.95)

Answers to Life's Questions—This book is an engaging sample of questions John-Roger has answered over the last 30+ years about Soul Transcendence, the spiritual nature of life, and practical spirituality. Covering subjects from angels and the souls of animals, to the Silent Ones and the Names of God, this book offers food for thought and nourishment for the soul.
(ISBN 189302007X, Paper, $7.95)

Forgiveness–The Key to the Kingdom—A collection of excerpts showing us how using forgiveness in many everyday situations can bring us closer to the awareness of our divinity.
(ISBN 0914829629, Paper, $12.95)

Dream Voyages—Is there a difference between dreaming and soul travel—or are they the same? In this ground-breaking volume, John-Roger explains the important difference between dreaming and night travel and its role in spiritual development.
(ISBN 0914829319, Paper, $12.95)

AUDIO MATERIALS

Spiritual Exercises—Walking with the Lord (Companion to the book *Spiritual Exercises — Walking with the Lord*). Four tapes with excerpts on spiritual exercises and a seminar by John-Roger. The enclosed booklet has the printed transcription of the excerpts and identifies the original source material.
(Available from MSIA; 4 audio cassettes, #3907, $30)

Inner Worlds of Meditation—A recorded set of spiritual exercises, the companion to the book *Inner Worlds of Meditation*.
(ISBN 0914829645, 3 CDs or 6 audio cassettes, $45)

Turning Points to Personal Liberation—John-Roger presents direct, insightful information outlining the causes and cures of hurt, anger, confusion, jealousy, feelings of separation and loneliness, and other limiting behaviors and beliefs that often block our happiness, success, and enjoyment. These tapes contain practical keys and wisdom for gaining greater acceptance, understanding, loving, freedom, and liberation.
(ISBN 0914829610, 6 audio cassettes, $45)

The Wayshower—Two cassette tapes and a booklet in which John-Roger tells about his life and awakening to the spiritual consciousness he now carries. A delightful mixture of funny stories John-Roger tells on himself and the profound message of the spiritual work he is here to do.
(Available from MSIA; 2 audio cassettes, #3901, $20)

Soul Journey through Spiritual Exercises—Three tapes and a booklet, including a spiritual exercises seminar, "Meditation for Soul Travel," and "HU Chant & Breathing Exercise," all conducted by John-Roger. You are your soul. There is no more important mission than awakening to your divine inheritance. The Soul Journey packet facilitates the trip.
(Available from MSIA; 3 audio cassettes, #3718, $25)

My Kingdom For a Horse—An extended version of John-Roger's "far memory" of obtaining horses for his spiritual teacher.
(Available from MSIA; audiotape #4018, $10)

Cathedral of the Soul—In a mini-seminar, John-Roger presents some keys to active meditation, to assist you to move back from yourself so that you may see yourself more clearly and realize your true reality. He speaks of communication with your high self through meditation. Then he takes you on a beautiful meditative journey to the cathedral of your soul.
(Available from MSIA; audiotape #3714, $10)

Nuclear Radiation from Ground Zero—From a place of off-the-wall humor, John-Roger asks us what price we are willing to pay to get out of a situation that is not working for us, and reminds us that we often must take a loss to make a gain.
(Available from MSIA; audiotape #7061, $10)

ONGOING STUDY

Soul Awareness Discourses—A Course In Soul Transcendence—Soul Awareness Discourses are designed to teach Soul Transcendence, which is becoming aware of yourself as a soul and as one with God, not as a theory but as a living reality. They are for people who want a consistent, time-proven approach to their spiritual unfoldment. The first year Discourse Kit includes 12 individual Discourses (one for each month of the year), a deluxe binder, a beautiful storage case, and resource material for tracking your spiritual growth and awareness. Topics include Realms of Light, Acceptance, The Law of Cause and Effect, and Responsibility, to name a few. Studying Discourses often leads to better health, greater wealth, more loving relationships, and, most important, knowing God as a living reality in your life.

A yearly set of Discourses is regularly $100. MSIA is offering the first year of Discourses at an introductory price of $50. Discourses come with a full, no-questions-asked, money-back guarantee. If at any time you decide this course of study is not right for you, return them and you will promptly receive a full refund.

(Available from MSIA: Order #5000, $50)

Contact Information

The Movement of Spiritual Inner Awareness (MSIA)
P.O. Box 513935, Los Angeles, CA 90051-1935
(800) 899-2665   www.msia.org